NOT GUILTY
EVERY TIME

NOT GUILTY EVERY TIME

Keys to Courtroom Victory

by

CHARLES C. HAGAN, Jr.

Copyright © 2004 by Charles C. Hagan, Jr.

All rights reserved
Printed in the United States of America
First Edition

No part of this publication may be reproduced or transmitted in any form or by any means, electronic or mechanical, including photocopy, recording, or any information storage and retrieval system, without prior written permission of the publisher except in case of brief quotations embodied in critical articles or reviews.

Grateful acknowledgment is made to the following for permission to reprint previously published materials: Stephen J. Adler: excerpt from The Jury: Trial and Error In The American Courtroom © 1994 by Stephen J. Adler (Random House) Reprinted by permission of the author.

Hagan, Jr. Charles C.
Not Guilty Every Time: Keys to Courtroom Victory
/Charles C. Hagan, Jr..--1st Ed.
p.cm
ISBN 0-9759490-0-4
Library of Congress Control Number: **2004108411**
1. Trial practice--United States 2. Jury-United States 3. Trial Advocacy 4. Lawyers--United States 5. Forensic Oratory

Published by Millennium Vision Press
First Printing June 2004

TABLE OF CONTENTS

Epigraph 6
Acknowledgments 7
About the Author 8

INTRODUCTION 9

A Jury Trial From Start To Finish 15
When The Jury Returns A Verdict 18

SECTION ONE: The Trial Process

Chapter 1 Jury Selection & Questions 19
Chapter 2 The Purpose of Opening Statements 27
Chapter 3 The Purpose of Closing Arguments 31
Chapter 4 Reasonable Doubt &
                 the Presumption of Innocence 35
Chapter 5 Twelve Pointers to Not Guilty 48

SECTION TWO: 12 Trials, 12 Wins, 12 Free Clients

CASE 1   Assault 1st 51
CASE 2   Sodomy 1st 61
CASE 3   Wanton Endangerment 1st 73
CASE 4   Grave Desecration & Criminal Mischief 85
CASE 5   Trafficking in Stolen Vehicles & Parts 97
CASE 6   Theft over $300 *($3,000* lawnmower) 109
CASE 7   Murder 117
CASE 8   Rape, Sodomy, Robbery 133
CASE 9   Trafficking in Cocaine 147
CASE 10 Trafficking in Cocaine 161
CASE 11 Assault 1st 171
CASE 12 Theft over $300 (computer monitors) 185

Tidbits for Closing Arguments 198

Glossary of Legal Definitions 204

SuggestedReadings 210

EPIGRAPH

As a practical matter the not-guilty person leaves the courthouse with all his freedoms and most of his privileges intact, while the guilty person goes to prison and, if he emerges, continues to suffer the consequences of having been found guilty. Depending on the nature and severity of his crime, he may be legally barred from voting or serving on a jury, denied occupational licenses, prevented from holding public offices, rejected for automobile insurance, or denied parental rights. Informally the stigma of a felony conviction can cause him countless other problems. Licensing boards, employers or landlords won't buy the excuse of a false accusation; the jury's verdict has determined the truth. Boxer Mike Tyson will live his life as a convicted rapist. Physician William Kennedy Smith will not. Their juries didn't just evaluate the government's proof; they wrote history.

The Jury: Trial And Error In The American Courtroom
Stephen J. Adler (Random House)
Reprinted by permission of the author

ACKNOWLEDGEMENTS

I give thanks to my GOD for gifting me with the ability to speak, communicate, and powers of persuasion. I am also deeply indebted and grateful to the following persons for their excellent and valuable help in completing this manuscript; Paul J. Mullins, Darwin Payne, Daryll Craft, and Phillip Taylor.

I have had a number of mentors over the years, and I would like to personally thank each of them for inspiring me to strive towards excellence. I am eternally grateful to all of my teachers and instructors over the years. I would like to say thanks to my pastor and mentor, Dr. Kevin Cosby, pastor of the St Stephen Church (Louisville,KY)

This book is dedicated to the memory of my father, Charles Threatt, who passed last year. In his memory and honor, this book is dedicated to his wife, Rita, to my brothers Hubert Hagan, Christopher Hagan, and Charles A. Threatt, and to my sisters Valerie McCamey, Carmella Threatt and Gloria Threatt, to my cousin , Anna Gray Coleman,and to all of my neices and nephews (ChelitaGray, P.J. Gray, Tisha Gray, Brandon Hagan, Kristen Hagan, LaNeisha Threatt, LaTeisha Brown, Kenneth Johnson, Tifany Threatt, and Joshua Threatt). I wholeheartedly dedicate it to my three sons, Byron, Bryant and Brinnon. I pray God's blessings on all of you!

This book is also dedicated to my longtime family pastor, Dr. James E. Miller of Lampton Baptist Church; good friends attorneys Paul J. Mullins, Denise Brown, Karl Price and Keith Brown (Alexandria, VA); longtime friends Courtney Long (Indianapolis, IN) John Govan (Columbia, SC), Sherman Bush, Lester Crayton, Cordell Stone, Joel Dansby, Raoul Cunningham, John Railey, LeGetano McCurley, Karl Mahaffey, Delores & Erica Ezell, Karl Wilson Sr and Karl Wilson Jr (Boo). I love all of you and will always be grateful for your continuing love and support.

ABOUT THE AUTHOR

Charles C. Hagan, Jr. has been a practicing attorney in Louisville, KY for over twenty-three years. A 1969 graduate of Louisville Male High School, he graduated from the University of Louisville (B.A. 1972) in three years with a major in political science. He also graduated from the Brandeis School of Law at the University of Louisville (J.D. 1975).

Charles is a former Upward Bound student, Who's Who Among Students in American Colleges and Universities (1972), a University of Kentucky CLEO graduate, and a three time Earl Warren Legal Training Scholarship recipient. He worked for the Louisville Urban League as Voter Registration Coordinator for two years and he directed two juvenile diversion and youth employment programs.

In 1982 Charles Hagan was nominated and acknowledged as one of the Outstanding Young Men of America. After nine months with the Jefferson District Public Defender's office, he began a private law practice in May 1980. The firm concentrates its practice in criminal defense, personal injury, wrongful death, and family law matters. Hagan is a member of the Louisville and Kentucky Bar Associations, has been listed in Martindale-Hubbell, is a voting member of the Association of Trial Lawyers of America, and was admitted to practice before the United States Supreme Court in July 1986.

Hagan is a highly organized, meticulously prepared, courtroom savvy, detail oriented, and aggressive criminal defense attorney who consistently achieves successful results for his clients. He delivers quality legal representation and wins numerous acquittals and dismissals for the clients he represents. Hagan has extensive experience in criminal law and a proven track record of successes. His motto is aggressive representation, effective advocacy, and gentle persuasion.

Hagan has been involved in numerous civic, community, and educational activities. He has served as a judge for the Moot Court competition at the Brandeis School of Law, and the National Mock Court Trial competition at Eastern Kentucky University. He served as Executive Director of the Midwest Missionary Baptist Youth Conference Inc. (1984-1988), and as a former Chapter Representative of the Kentuckiana Chapter of the Gospel Music Workshop of America Inc. He is a member and trustee of the St. Stephen Baptist Church.

Hagan lives in Louisville with his three sons, Brinnon, Bryant and Byron. He is an avid reader, fine art collector, loves to travel, enjoys gospel music, and dabbles in home interior decoration in his spare time.

INTRODUCTION

*Jury **ACQUITS** wife's former husband in shooting of new boyfriend*

***HUNG JURY** in case of soldier accused of sodomy of six year old girl*

*Assault on narcotics officers with tire jack ends in **NOT GUILTY** verdict*

*465 tombstones destroyed in Eastern Cemetery, jury **ACQUITS** all 6 defendants*

*Jail inmate **ACQUITTED** of trafficking in stolen vehicles for renting Avis cars to fellow inmates*

*Jury takes less than twenty five minutes finds defendant **NOT GUILTY** of murder*

***HUNG JURY** in rape, sodomy, **NOT GUILTY** of robbery*

*Trafficking in cocaine and diazepam Jury sets **DEFENDANT FREE***

***NOT GUILTY VERDICT** for defendant in brawl at motorcycle c*

*City of Louisville employee **NOT GUILTY** of stealing city lawnmower worth $3,000*

*Jury **ACQUITS** former Ryder Logistics employee of theft of $500,000 of computer monitors*

    The above could have been the newspaper headlines for each of the 12 jury trials portrayed in this book. Sometimes the judge reads the verdict: "The jury has found the defendant not guilty of all charges." Sometimes the foreperson of the jury reads the verdict: "We the jury find the defendant not guilty of counts # 1, 2 and 3." And sometimes the clerk of the court is asked to read the verdict. No matter who reads theverdict or the jury decision, those words and the above headlines are like "magic" to the eyes and ears of every criminal defense attorney. They are what criminal defense attorneys love to see and hear at the end of every jury trial.

Not guilty verdicts or a hung jury must be the goal of every defense lawyer that takes a case to jury trial. This book is about twelve cases that went to jury trial and resulted in "twelve wins"; nine not guilty verdicts, two hung jury verdicts, one split verdict (not guilty and hung jury), and one verdict on a lesser included offense, and which was admitted and asked for by the defendant. Eleven of these cases were tried by me, and one was tried by my partner Attorney Paul J. Mullins.

My name is Charles C. Hagan, Jr. and I am a practicing attorney and primarily known in the Louisville community as a criminal defense attorney. I represent people charged with the violation of one or more of the criminal laws of the Commonwealth of Kentucky. I have represented defendants on every type of serious felony charge including; murder, manslaughter, assault, robbery, wanton endangerment, kidnapping, sexual assault crimes, theft, grave desecration, criminal mischief, domestic violence, drug trafficking and possession, and many other serious misdemeanor and felony offenses.

In over twenty three years of practice, I have represented thousands of individuals on misdemeanor and felony charges in both state and federal courts. The majority of criminal defendants have their cases disposed of by guilty plea resulting in jail time, fines, restitution payments, probation, and conditionally discharged time. The cases of some defendants get diverted, a few get dismissed, and some defendants serve time in jail or prison.

Criminal cases sometimes do not settle because a prosecutor decides that the case is not appropriate for either a plea or other resolution. Another reason cases do not settle is the offer given to the defendant is unfair and is rejected by the defendant, if he is representing himself. If the defendant is represented by a lawyer, the lawyer may advise him to reject the prosecution's offer of settlement. When a case cannot be disposed of or settled in one of the above ways, it is usually set for a jury trial.

NOT GUILTY EVERY TIME is the title of this book, but I certainly do not mean to imply that I have won every case I have ever tried. Lawyers who regularly defend criminal cases will quickly tell you that no one wins all of their cases or trials. Famed Harvard law school professor and appellate Attorney Allen M. Dershowitz, says that "the truth is that most criminal defendants are, in fact, guilty." (Note1) **Bureau of Justice Statistics for 1998 reveal that 9 of 10 defendants with**

either publicly appointed or private counsel were found guilty (5% to 6% by trial). The acquittal rate for defendants whose cases go to trial in the nation's 75 largest counties is a scant 1.3% for publicly appointed counsel and 1.6% for private counsel.(Note 2)

In compiling the research for this book, I was pleasantly surprised to find that as of the writing of this book, I have compiled an 80% success rate of all criminal cases I have taken to jury trial. This record also includes a hung jury on at least three occasions, one misdemeanor verdict, and one mistrial (which was subsequently dismissed with prejudice). And yes, I have passed the Irving Younger test.(Note 3)

NOT GUILTY EVERY TIME is a primer and is aimed at the newly admitted and inexperienced, attorney waiting to try that first criminal case. It is also aimed at the novice, veteran, civil attorney, or law professor who has never put a jury in the box.

Law school teaches writing, law, theory, evidence, and procedure. Law school also helps future barristers to acquire sharp legal minds. However, it is years of practice and numerous courtroom experiences that enable lawyers to fine tune and perfect litigation skills.

"It requires a number of actual courtroom experiences before many lawyers understand that the advocate's role is to be an effective communicator and persuader in support of a point of view." (note 4)

Acquiring plenty of trial experiences in a variety of criminal cases takes time. Time is in short commodity with the new lawyer. Perfecting litigation skills and gaining valuable courtroom experiences is often years in the making, and there is a gap which exists for the new lawyer. One of the ways to gain those experiences, perfect those skills, and to close that gap is to watch and learn from experienced trial lawyers in civil and criminal cases.

There are plenty of very good to excellent attorneys in my community that regularly defend and prosecute criminal cases on a regular basis. A few of the names that come to mind, and whom I have watched and admired over the years include, the late Frank Haddad and Joe Glass. I have also marveled at the incredible trial skills of Bart Adams, Frank Mascagni, Samuel Manly, Frank Jewell, and Don Majors, to name just a few. I have been duly impressed and learned a lot from watching civil attorneys such as brothers Gary Hillerich & Ron Hillerich, Tom Conway and Dennis Clare. I also like to watch different prosecutors and have been impressed by current prosecutors Carol Cobb, ex-Commonwealth Attorneys Joe Gutman, Keith Kamenish, and John W. Stewart. These are just a few of the top notch trial attorneys that I have watched over the years. I have learned something from every one of the lawyers on the above list.

The above lawyers are always well prepared and organized, and not afraid to share their knowledge and experiences with others who are looking for similar success. Watching these excellent lawyers and advocates try civil and criminal cases over the years has helped me gain me a solid working knowledge of how to try a civil or a criminal case, sharpened my advocacy and litigation skills, and made me a better trial attorney. I urge you to gain priceless, practical, and valuable lessons by watching other experienced attorneys try cases.

Numerous texts on the market deal with high profile cases, celebrity clients, and celebrity lawyers. However there are actually very few books to help the novice and inexperienced attorney take a criminal trial from start to finish in the early stages of their legal practices and careers. Many of the texts on the market use sample openings and sample closings. This book is intended to address the needs of that group of attorneys, and is filled with verbatim voir dire questions, opening statements, and closing arguments from real cases that went to jury trial.

My goal is that the tactics, strategies, and insight gained from these twelve cases will help new lawyers sharpen their advocacy skills, manage a trial from start to finish, select a fair and impartial jury, deliver effective opening statements, draft and deliver winning closing arguments, and improve the chances for a jury to say "not guilty" every time. I have not attempted to cover all of the areas of trial advocacy such as cross-examination, witness preparation, exhibit handling and so forth. There are plenty of valuable resources and aids in these areas.

The cases in this book include the offenses of assault first degree (2 cases), sodomy first degree, wanton endangerment first degree, violation of graves, criminal mischief first degree, trafficking in stolen vehicles and parts, theft by unlawful taking over $300 (2 cases), murder, rape, robbery, kidnapping, trafficking in controlled substances (2 cases and 2 defendants). Five of the defendants in these twelve cases were also charged as (PFO's) persistent felony offenders, meaning they would receive additional time if convicted. In those five cases, the defendants exercised their Fifth Amendment Right, did not take the stand and testify, and still walked away with their liberty and freedom.

The results in the twelve cases in this book are:

NOT GUILTY VERDICTS (all charges)	9
HUNG JURY (all charges)	1
HUNG JURY/NOT GUILTY	1
GUILTY on lesser offense (admitted)	1

Also included in this book are (16) voir dire questions, (10) opening statements, and (12) closing arguments. This book also includes a chapter on how to use the "presumption of innocence" and "proof beyond a reasonable doubt" to get a win for your client. Included in that chapter are **Twelve Ways To Use The Presumption of Innocence and Twelve Ways To Use The Proof Beyond A Reasonable Doubt Standard.** Finally the book includes **Twelve Pointers To Not Guilty Every Time** and **Tidbits for Closing Arguments.**

The voir dire questions, opening statements, and closing arguments were taken verbatim from the transcripts, audiotapes and videotapes still available. A small amount of editing has been done for purposes of clarity and where the original source was unclear. For reasons of privacy and confidentiality, the names of all defendants and abuse victims have been changed to either a "fictitious name" or to "defendant" or "victim."

The ideas and themes in these opening statements, voir dire questions, and closing arguments are tried, tested, and proven. Every criminal defense attorney should strive to get a win every time they put a jury in the box. A "win" is a not guilty verdict, a hung jury, or a verdict on a lesser included offense, usually a misdemeanor and often resulting in little or no jail or prison time. This office had a recent streak of nine "wins" in a row in criminal felony jury trials in the Jefferson Circuit Courts in Louisville, KY.

New lawyers should never feel that a victory is either guaranteed or automatic. Success is generated by hard work, painstaking and detailed preparation, intensity, creativity, and perseverance. Remember what Emily Couric says about the top ten litigators in the country;

"Overconfidence is an invitation to fail. Too much confidence dulls attention to detail, attentiveness in trial, and the ability to respond quickly to changing circumstances. Because the flip side of winning is losing, love of one is often driven by fear of the other." (note 5)

I hope this book will serve generations of future lawyers and advocates. May the Lord God bless you real good!

Charles C. Hagan Jr.

TRIAL BY JURY

"The Anglo-American jury is a remarkable political institution...It recruits twelve laymen, chosen at random from the widest population; it convenes them for the purpose of the particular trial; it entrusts them with great official powers of decision; it permits them to carry on deliberations in secret and to report out their final judgment without giving reasons for it; and after thier momentary service to the state has been completed, it orders them to disband and return to private life... The jury is thus by definition an exciting experience in the conduct of serious human affairs that virtually from its inception, has been the subject of deep controversy."

The American Jury,
Harry Kalven, Jr and Hans Zeisel
(1966), pp 1-32.

*

"I consider trial by jury as the only anchor ever yet imagined by man, by which a government can be held to the principles of its constitution."

Thomas Jefferson

*

"All of the privileges of a complete and free society are guaranteed and reinforced by the fact that all citizens have a right, no matter who their opposition, to have their rights heard before a jury of their peers. This secures to America its unique form of democratic government and the freedomes that abound."

Alexis de Tocqueville

A CRIMINAL JURY TRIAL
From Start to Finish

Arrest or citation
Indictment or information
Arraignment
Pretrial Conference

Case Set For Jury Trial

Pretrial Conference

Pretrial Motions

Separation of Witnesses

Jury Selection

Swearing in of Jury by Court

Opening Statement by Prosecutor

Opening Statement by the defense
   (may be waived or reserved until defense case)

Prosecution's evidence (case in chief)
     Cross-examination by the defense

Defense motion for directed verdict or to dismiss
     (usually overruled by the judge)

Defendant's evidence (case in chief)
     Cross-examination by the prosecution

Rebuttal

Renewal of defendant's motion to dismiss or for directed verdict (usually overruled by the judge)

Instructions of law prepared in consultation with defense, prosecution and the Court

Instructions of law read by Court

(copies sometimes provided to jurors so they can read along)

Closing Argument by defense

Closing Argument by prosecution

(In some jurisdictions the prosecution goes first, followed by the defense, with prosecution rebuttal)

13th or 14th jurors randomly struck by the Court

Sheriff sworn

Jury Deliberations

Verdict

Must be unanimous in all states except Oregon and Louisiana which allow for 10 of 12 votes for conviction

If defendant is acquitted (found not guilty) the defendant is usually discharged, and if in custody is released the same day

Poll of jury
    (each juror is asked if the verdict is their verdict)

Sentencing (if defendant is found guilty)
    (sometimes done on the same day, but usually set for a different day, after a presentence investigation is ordered)

Post-trial motions

Notice of Appeal

JURY TRIAL PROTECTIONS

1. Article III, Section 2, Clause 3, United States Constitution

2. 5th Amendment, United States Constitution (due process)

3. 6th Amendment, United States Constitution (criminal jury trial)

4. 14th Amendment, United States Constitution, (due process and

equal protection)

IMPORTANT RIGHTS IN THE AMERICAN CRIMINAL JUSTICE SYSTEM

1. Right to a speedy and public trial

2. Right to a trial by an impartial jury

3. Right to notice of the charges

4. Right to confront and cross examine the state's witnesses

5. Right to compulsory process to secure the attendance of witnesses

6. Right to effective assistance of counsel

7. Right to counsel in non-trial situations

8. Right to refuse to testify or remain silent

9. Right to have jury determine guilt unanimously and beyond a reasonable doubt as to each element of each offense charge

10. Right to self representation

When the Jury Returns Its Verdict

Scene 1 (routinely played out in courtrooms all over the country every day where there are about 150,000 trials a year). After announcing that they have reached a verdict, the Court summons all of the attorneys, the defendant, and other court personnel back into the courtroom. Once all have assembled, the Sheriff brings the jury into the Courtroom and they take their seats in the jury box

Judge: Ladies and gentlemen of the jury, have you reached a verdict?

Foreperson: Yes, Your honor, we have

Judge: May I examine the verdict?

Foreperson: Yes you may your honor

Judge: Will you hand the verdict to the sheriff

[Sheriff gets the verdict from the foreperson and hands it to the Judge. The judge examines the verdict form for correctness and proper signatures and hands the verdict form back to the sheriff to give to the foreperson, or gives it to the clerk, or the judge may read it]

Judge: Will the defendant and his counsel please rise and face the jury

Judge: Foreperson you may read your verdict

Foreperson: We the jury find the defendant not guilty

Judge: Ladies and gentlemen is that your verdict?
[All jurors nod heads]

Judge: Does anyone request a poll of the jury?

CHAPTER 1

JURY SELECTION & JURY QUESTIONS

One of the most important parts of a criminal jury trial is known of as *"voir dire"* or the selection of the jury. *Voir dire* is a French phrase that means "to say truly or true talk."

Voir dire is a black art of getting information to rid the jury of those most likely to hurt you, or help your opponent, and at the same time, get information about jurors which will later help you to construct the best arguments to persuade them.(note 6)

The often stated purposes of jury selection are:

1. Help select jurors whom you can actually persuade to accept your version of the facts.

2. Remove or "deselect" jurors who seem unfavorable, and who seem inclined to help your opponent score a guilty verdict.

3. Obtain information about jurors attitudes and opinions without offending any juror (note 7)

4. Establish rapport with jurors

5. Lay out the themes, facts, and information about your client and orient the jury to your version of the case

In many jurisdictions the judge conducts the entire examination of the prospective jurors. In those jurisdictions, the attorney is often allowed to submit written questions for the judge to ask of the prospective jurors. In some jurisdictions, both the court and counsel question the jury. However, in most counties in Kentucky, lawyers are permitted to ask individual questions of the prospective jury panel.

I will not attempt to discuss the different rules and policies on jury selection, or how the judge's role varies from jurisdiction to jurisdiction. However, it should be stressed and emphasized that every lawyer must become familiar with the applicable law and statutes, rules of procedures, local court practices, and the preference of the individual judges for the jurisdiction where the case is to be tried.

I have included a set of juror questions that I use to prepare for every criminal case that my office takes to a jury trial. These will often be supplemented by the peculiarities of each individual case. The major themes of the case must be highlighted and carefully woven throughout the trial, and must begin during jury selection, and continue through opening statements and closing argument. Themes that I touch on during jury selection always include the following; burden of proof, the presumption of innocence, deciding the case on facts and Instructions, following the law, actions of the attorneys, commitment to be fair and do justice, non-testifying defendant, commitment to your own verdict, dealing with prejudice and sympathy, and reasonable doubt. The same concepts and themes must be highlighted again during summation or closing argument.

SAMPLE JURY QUESTIONS

By now you know my name is Charles Curtis Hagan, Jr. and I represent the defendant in this case. As I ask you questions, if you feel a question has reference to you, please respond by raising your hand.

Does everyone understand that the purpose of jury selection or *"voir dire"* is not to embarrass you or to make you feel uncomfortable, but to help us select the twelve jurors that will be impartial and fair to both sides?

This is a criminal case where the Commonwealth would like to send the defendant to the penitentiary for up to 20 years. And as a result of that certain protections are afforded to the defendant. And I will go over those protections.

PRESUMPTION OF INNOCENCE

Does everyone understand that the defendant comes into this courthouse, and into this very courtroom with the presumption of innocence, and the defendant is presumed innocent throughout this trial?

Is there anyone here who feels that just because a person is charged with a crime, he or she must have done something wrong, or they wouldn't be here?

INDICTMENT NOT EVIDENCE

Does everyone understand that the indictment returned by the Jefferson County Grand Jury is not evidence? It has no weight, it is not evidence now, during the presentation of evidence, or during your deliberations in this case?

BURDEN OF PROOF

When we talk about the burden of proof, what we mean is that the defendant doesn't have to prove anything. In fact, we don't have to put on any evidence or call any witnesses, or cross examine any of the prosecutions witnesses.

Does everyone understand that we can sit over here like a bump on a log, and do nothing? And still the Commonwealth must prove to you that the defendant is guilty beyond a reasonable doubt, from its evidence and its evidence alone. That is their burden. If we were to take a vote right now, how would you vote? Does everyone understand that your vote would have to be "not guilty"? *Pick some people at random to ask this question.*

REASONABLE DOUBT

The defendant doesn't have to prove his innocence, but the Commonwealth has to prove his guilt and prove it beyond a reasonable doubt. Does everyone understand this?

Does everyone understand that it is the Commonwealth's responsibility and duty to prove each and every element of each of the offenses of which he is charged beyond a reasonable doubt.

At the end of this trial, the judge is going to give you an Instruction of law on reasonable doubt. I am not permitted to define reasonable doubt, but I can say that if the Commonwealth, represented by this prosecutor, doesn't paint the complete picture for you, and only convinces you that the defendant is or appears to be guilty, or engaged in what appeared to be a [*whatever crime applies*] drug transaction, or is probably guilty, or is possibly guilty, or that there is a strong suspicion of guilt, the law requires you to find the defendant not guilty. In other words, reasonable doubt is the standard against which you will test all the evidence in this case. Does everyone understand this?

Does anyone feel that the criminal standard of "beyond a reasonable doubt" is too high of a standard for the state to have to prove? Does anyone feel that because of this standard, too many criminals go free? *Pick out some members and talk to them.*

INNOCENT PERSONS GOING TO PRISON

Often we pick up newspaper and the headline reads, "Defendant Is Arrested" and the drift of the story is that the person was obviously guilty, but he goes free on a technicality. Then, I want to talk about another type of headline, "Innocent Person Released After X Number of Years in Prison."

I want you to compare in your mind the difference in those two. Is there anybody here that doesn't believe that the latter one is more serious?

FOLLOWING THE LAW

Does everyone understand that when a jury finds someone not guilty, when the prosecution fails to prove its case, and you say not guilty, you are still following and upholding the law? Is there anyone here that would feel bad if that happened?

OBJECTIONS DURING TRIAL

You understand that during a trial it is necessary for both sides to make what we call objections. And when we make objections, it doesn't mean that there is something we want to hide or keep from you, but there is a legal reason for us to do so. And in doing so, we are carrying out our duties as both lawyers and officers of the Court. Does each of you understand that you can't hold it against my client if you think I am objecting too much?

CROSS EXAMINATION

Each of us also has a duty to cross examine the other side's witnesses, and to do so vigorously and completely. And many times we might run into witnesses that are not being truthful, or telling a complete story, and that might be hostile. You understand you can't use it as evidence, when we carry out our duties, and cross examine witnesses vigorously and completely?

STATE HAS TWICE AS MANY WITNESSES

In this case, as in most criminal cases, there will be three or even four times as many witnesses for the State than there are for the defendant. You wouldn't accept the combined testimony of the prosecutions witnesses just because there are more of them? In other words this is not a numbers game of who has the largest number of witnesses.

DEFENDANT MAY NOT TESTIFY

Now everyone understands that the prosecution must present its case first, and then the defendant, if he desires, may put on evidence, and is permitted to take the stand and testify himself. All of us, including the defendant, have the right not to take that stand and testify. And the defendant, just like the rest of us, can exercise what is known of as his Fifth Amendment Right or the right against self incrimination, and decide not to testify. And a lot of times the decision on whether the defendant will testify cannot be made until late in a trial. So I can't tell you at this point whether or not the defendant will testify.

Knowing all of this, and that the defendant might not testify, is there anyone who would consider his failure to take the stand and testify as an indication of his guilt?

Once again, the only story that needs to be told is that told by the State or the Commonwealth. The law doesn't allow you to use it against him if he chooses to exercise that fundamental and constitutional right and not take the stand. In other words, his silence cannot be used as evidence against him. Is there anyone who does not understnd this?

JUDGE THE CASE ON EVIDENCE, INSTRUCTIONS OF LAW

This case can be judged on only two things; the evidence that will come from this chair, and the law which will be given to you by the judge as Instructions at the close of this case.

What we are talking about is being fair and impartial, listening to the facts of this particular case, and not trying to compare it or size it up with something you might have read in a book, seen in a play or movie, or watched on television.

UNANSWERED QUESTIONS

Is there any question that has not been asked of you that would indicate if seated as a juror in this case, that you could not be fair and impartial, and that you would be unduly and improperly prejudiced, or that you have a known or unknown bias, or that you favor either party in this case prior to hearing any evidence and the Instructions of law?

SIMILAR INCIDENTS OR EXPERIENCES

Merely because you had a similar incident or experience, would that cause you any problems to sit in this case, listen to the evidence, and return a fair and impartial verdict, or would that cause you to lean to one side or the other?

Taking into consideration the fact that you have had this type of prior experience, don't you feel that you would be better able to serve as a juror on a different kind of case?

Is there anyone here who has been charged with a drug crime? What about any relatives or friends? Would you like to tell me about that in front of the judge?

Does anyone here have any special education or training in sexual assault or abuse cases. What about your relatives or friends?

PREVIOUS JURY SERVICE,
WORK IN THE COURT SYSTEM

Has anyone on the panel ever served previously as a juror? Was it a criminal or civil case? Was a verdict reached in the case?

Has anyone here ever served as a foreman, forewoman or a foreperson on a jury? Was it a civil or criminal case?

Has anyone here ever been employed by the court or the legal system?

Has anyone here ever been employed by a law enforcement or police agency, or as a police officer, or as a security guard?

For all of those who have served as a juror or foreperson, is there anything about your previous jury experience that would make you lean either for the prosecution or the defense in this case?

PROMISE TO BE FAIR

Finally, if selected to serve, as a juror in this case, will you all agree that you will render a fair and impartial verdict in the case, and base your decision solely on the evidence that's presented, and the law as given to you by the Court in the Instructions, even if you disagree with that law?

      I'm sure if you're selected you will do a fair and honorable job as a juror

CHAPTER 2

THE PURPOSE OF OPENING STATEMENTS

The jury has been selected, sworn in, and seated in the jury box. The trial moves to Opening Statements, first by the prosecution, and then (unless waived) by the defense. They are often called Opening Arguments and, according to the rules in most jurisdictions, they should be done without arguing the case. Argument will usually draw an objection from the prosecution. Argument or summation is supposed to be saved for the closing argument.

The real purpose of opening statements is to show what you expect the evidence to be. Over the years, I have heard and listened to various explanations and descriptions, of Opening Statements. I have collected a number of them from both the defense and prosecution. These are the most popular ones, and they can often be used alone or in combination with others for an explanation to the jury of this phase of the trial. I cite nine for your perusal and review.

1. A **roadmap** to show what direction the prosecution and the defense are headed.

2. A **movie preview** to whet your appetite for coming attractions.

3. A **blueprint** and a layout of the facts so the jury can follow the evidence and make the right decision.

4. A **bird's eye view** of the evidence as it is introduced, usually piecemeal and often out of order.(note 8)

5. A **summary** of what you expect the evidence will be make it easier for both the judge and the jury to follow the case.

6. The **lenses** through which jurors grind and view the evidence.(note 9)

7. Projecting a **winning attitude** and motivate the jury to find

for your client.

8. Explaining the **conclusions** and the verdict you want the jury to reach.(note 10)

9. The **explanation** by the attorney at the beginning of what will be proved during the trial. It is a factual presentation and not an argument.(note 11)

> Fredric Levin suggests that opening statements are among the most important, but often overlooked parts of a good trial strategy. An opening statement, he says, "makes it possible to capture and hold the jury's attention, puts you in control of the case immediately, gets the jury on your side, and may very well put your opponent off balance for the rest of the trial." (note 12)
>
> Once you have prepared your opening statement, test it against the "Opening Statement Critique" advanced in *Trialbook Second Edition.* (note 13)

Does the opening statement tell what happened?

Does the opening statement tell the fact finder why to find for the client?

Does the opening statement make the fact finder want to find for the client?

Does the opening statement tell how to find for the client?

Does the opening statement have a structure that is clear and simple?

Is the opening statement consistent with what will be proved and what will be argued in summation?

The opening statement must be delivered with the utmost confidence and authority, since statistics indicate a majority of jurors reach a decision by the end of opening argument, and never change their opinions about the case.

> *The opening is THE trial. Approximately 80% of jurors reach a "preliminary" decision by the end of opening statements, and never change their minds. Because it is the time when most persuasion occurs, the opening*

MUST be better PREPARED, and better REHEARSED than any part of the trial." (note 14)

You must believe in your own client's case before trying to convince the jurors to believe in it. You must convince the jury that not only do you believe in your case, but you believe in their ability to be fair, render justice, and to return a verdict of not guilty for your client.

CHAPTER 3

THE PURPOSE OF CLOSING ARGUMENT

The trial is over. Both sides have presented their evidence and the Instructions of Law have been prepared. The judge reads the Instructions to the jury, many of whom are reading along with copies given to them by the sheriff. In some jurisdictions, the judge will not give out copies, but will send the original to the jury room, along with the other trial exhibits.

The jury trial process now moves to the final stage and what is known of and commonly referred to as "closing argument." It is also sometimes called summation, argument, or closing statements.

The defense usually goes first and the prosecution goes last. However, in some jurisdictions the prosecution goes first, the defense goes second, and the prosecution is given a last chance for rebuttal. Most judges limit the amount of time for "closing argument" and decide it in conference and with the lawyers at the beginning or at the end of the case.

The purposes of closing argument are:

1. **Summarize** both the testimonial and documentary evidence

2. **Draw** together all facts and the reasonable inferences from the record

3. **Sharpen** and clarify the issues and **convince** the jury to find in your client's favor

4. **Present** theories so the fact finder can make the right decision in the case

5. **Sell** the jury on the truth and justice of your client's case.

"Closing argument is the lawyer's final opportunity to give perspective, meaning, and context to the evidence introduced throughout a lengthy trial. It is the last chance for the lawyer to forcefully

communicate his position to the jury, to convince them of why his version of the "truth" is correct." (note 15)

Some of the other purposes for closing argument are; to give arguments to the leaders on the jury to use in persuading other jurors to come with them or to switch sides, to solidify wavering jurors, and to make sure favorable jurors understand what they must do to give you the verdict you want and have asked for.

Closing argument is a fundamental part of basic due process rights. Closing argument is considered an integral part of effective representation and assistance of counsel, and it is therefore mandatory for the criminal defense attorney to give a persuasive closing argument on behalf of their client. The waiving of closing argument should be considered as gambling of the highest stakes, with a client's freedom and liberty hanging in the balance.

How does an attorney prepare to summarize days, weeks, and sometimes months of trial testimony and evidence, and do it in a very restricted time frame?

My approach to closing argument has been consistent and straightforward over the years. Preparation for closing argument begins when the case comes into my office, and when it is determined that the case will have to be tried.

I often think about the words and the phraseology that will persuade a jury and get a win for my client. Whenever a thought, idea, or theme comes to mind, I jot it down on a piece of paper, place it into the clients file, and into the trial notebook that I have prepared for the case.

As the trial grows nearer and I actually begin to focus on the case, I will occasionally test out ideas and themes while in my office, driving my car, and during my leisure activities. My target for each closing argument is thirty to forty minutes, with the average being twenty to twenty five minutes. A very good text with eighteen hints for summation is by Henry G. Miller, Esq. and titled *On Trial: Lessons From A Lifetime In The Courtroom.* (note 16)

GUIDELINES FOR WINNING CLOSING ARGUMENTS

1. Be yourself and be honest, sincere, trustworthy, and credible

2. Exhibit confidence in yourself and your client's case

3. Choose a theme and a basic defense for the entire case

4. Start early and create a trial notebook including all the major sections and parts of the trial

5. Review previous cases and closings to see if there are any similarities and fact patterns you can use from other cases.

6. Stress the commitments obtained during jury selection

7. Weave the instructions with the facts in the record and place special emphasis upon the instructions

8. Show how the instructions mesh with the evidence in the record and how they favor your client

9. Recite the opening statement promises made and kept by you

10. Review opening statement promises made and broken by the government

11. Emphasize and review the evidence and the testimony, zeroing in on key witness testimony

12. Make sure your statements of fact are backed up by solid evidence in the record

13. Use the evidence in the record over and over again. If possible, get a copy of the previous day's video record or transcripts and quote verbatim from them

15. Explain the criminal standard of proof beyond a reasonable doubt and the presumption of innocence

16. Show the jury the consequences of a guilty verdict for your client and his family. See the "EPIGRAPH" in the front of this book

17. Ask the jury to find for your client by returning a not guilty verdict

18. Be courteous and thank the jury again for their patience, attentiveness, and commitment

If you consistently follow these principles and guidelines, writing a closing argument will become much easier. After writing or outlining your closing, you need to rehearse, rehearse, and rehearse again. Practice does make perfect. Practice it until you are able to deliver it with confidence, enthusiasm, and believability. Practice until you are able to deliver it with only glances at your notes. Act as if you own the courtroom, because in fact you really do. Make sure that your body language, eye contact, and voice are all polished for maximum effectiveness.

One of my favorite books and one I would highly recommend to the new and novice lawyer is *How to Argue and Win Every Time* by Gerry Spence. (note 16) He points out that we all have been conditioned against making the winning argument and he goes on to say "by the time the young lawyers face their first jury, they have doubtless had the winning argument crushed out of them by professors who have never tried a case." He then goes on to point out his "Ten Laws of Arguing According To Gerry Spence" and includes three I always remember and use; (1) everyone is capable of making the winning argument, (2) wining is getting what we want and helping others to get what they want, and (3) learning words are a weapon and can be used hostilely in combat.(note 17)

Watch complete trials, jury selection, opening statements, and the closing arguments from other real cases. Learn tricks of the trade from experienced prosecutors, civil litigators, and criminal defense lawyers. You will learn more from doing these things than from any textbooks or manuals. You will learn different styles, varied approaches, and countless other techniques from seasoned and veteran attorneys that will help to improve your advocacy and litigation skills.

It must be priority number one to be the best criminal defense lawyer. Only then will you be true to your oath as an advocate and defender!

CHAPTER 4

THE PRESUMPTION OF INNOCENCE & PROOF BEYOND A REASONABLE DOUBT

Seasoned criminal defense attorneys know that most criminal cases settle themselves, a few fall through the cracks and have to be tried, and a few are not worth the time and should be dealt away. Bad cases are those in which the prosecution has some damaging evidence; your client has made a damaging admission; or the evidence and the law are against you and no amount of creative advocacy will save your client from a criminal conviction. The other cases (the good ones) are those that present the greatest challenges to you as an advocate. They are weak on the facts, close on the law, or those in which the prosecution has serious evidentiary problems, and is not willing to cut a deal you can live with.

You must be prepared to take the good cases to trial, and the two tools that you can often use to your advantage are the presumption of innocence and proof beyond a reasonable a reasonable doubt.

The presumption of innocence is the principle that everyone who is accused of a criminal offense is presumed to be innocent until proven guilty. If is often defined as follows (note 18):

> *The indictment or formal charge against any person is not evidence of guilt. Indeed, the person is presumed by the law to be innocent. The law does not require a person to prove his innocence or produce any evidence at all. The government has the burden of proving a person guilty beyond a reasonable doubt, and if it fails to do so the person is (so far as the law is concerned) not guilty.*

The presumption of innocence is the most fundamental principle of the American criminal justice system and of most democratic countries throughout the world. It is also considered an important and integral part of international human rights law. This principle was declared in Article 11 of the United Nations Universal Declaration on Human Rights (December 10, 1948) and is stated:

> "Everyone charged with a penal offense has the right to be presumed innocent until proven guilty according to law in a public trial at which he has all the guarantees necessary for his defence." (note 19)

These principles can also be found and were established in Article 6 (2) of the Council of Europe's Convention for the Protection of Human Rights and Fundamental Freedoms (ECHR),

> "Everyone charged with a criminal offense shall be presumed innocent until proven guilty according to law." (note 20)

This principle is a cornerstone of the American, Canadian, Australian, and British criminal justice systems, and is inextricably linked to the principle of proof beyond a reasonable doubt. Both principles insure that no innocent person is ever convicted of a criminal offense. The judge and jury must both treat a defendant as being innocent.

The presumption of innocence begins when a person enters the criminal justice system (usually at the time of arrest) and is charged with a criminal offense. It continues through the trial and into the jury room until the jury begins its deliberations. The presumption is only done away with when all twelve jurors are convinced beyond a reasonable doubt that the government has met its burden of proof and established every element of each crime charged.

The goal of the American criminal justice system is a fair trial for every individual. It isoften said that it is better that five, ten, fifty or more guilty persons go free than for one innocent person to be convicted or put to death. Blackstone's Commentaries (1753-1756) also says that *"the law holds it is better that ten guilty persons escape than that one innocent suffer."* (note 21)

That principle can be found in a 1895 United States Supreme Court decision in *Coffin v. United States*, 156 U.S. 432, 15 S.Ct. 394 (1895). In *Coffin*, the Court said that the presumption goes back past England, ancient Greece and Rome, and even to Deuteronomy. In that case the Court said that at the request of a defendant, the Court must not only instruct on the prosecutions burden of proof—that a defendant may not be convicted unless the government has proven his guilt beyond a reasonable doubt—but the Court must also instruct on the presumption of innocence—by informing the jury that a defendant is presumed innocent. The Court wrote:

> *The principle that there is a presumption of innocence in favor of the accused is the undoubted law, axiomatic and elementary, and its enforcement lies at the foundation of the administration of our criminal law.* (note 22)

I will suggest twelve ways in which a lawyer can use the presumption of innocence to help persuade the jury to return a not guilty verdict for their client.

TWELVE WAYS TO USE THE PRESUMPTION OF INNOCENCE

1. The entire burden of persuasion rests on the government.

2. The burden never shifts to the defendant at any stage of the proceedings.

3. The indictment is not evidence and cannot be used in any way as evidence of the defendant's guilt.

4. The defendant may exercise his or her right and not testify, and the fact that he or she did not testify may not be used against them.

5. The defendant is not required to call any witnesses, produce any evidence or challenge any of the state's evidence or witnesses, or put on any defense(s) at all.

6. The presumption of innocence starts at the beginning of the trial and carries all through the trial until the jury deliberations.

7. Both the judge and the jury must presume that the defendant is not guilty through all stages of the proceedings.

8. The judge must inform the jury of the defendants presumption of innocence.

9. If the jury were to take a vote prior to any testimony or evidence, or prior to the conclusion of the entire case, and before any deliberations, their vote would have to be not guilty.

10. The jury must find the defendant guilty beyond a reasonable doubt of every element of each crime of which he or she is charged.

11. **The presumption is only done away with when all**

twelve jurors are convinced beyond a reasonable doubt of the defendants guilt.

12. The presumption of innocence serves to prevent oppression by the government and to protect against unfounded criminal charges and arbitrary action by magistrates and judges.

The second principle, "**proof beyond a reasonable doubt**" has often been defined as; "a real doubt, based upon reason and common sense after careful and impartial consideration of all the evidence, or lack of evidence, in a case."
In the O.J. Simpson case, Judge Ito gave the jury the following definition of reasonable doubt;

It is not a mere possible doubt because everything relating to human affairs is open to some possible or imaginary doubt. It is that state of the case, which after the entire comparison and consideration of all the evidence, leaves the minds of the jurors in that conditions that they cannot say they feel an abiding conviction about the truth of the charge. (note 23)

Every defendant in the United States of America charged with a criminal offense has each of the following constitutional rights:

1. The 5th amendment right against self incrimination

2. The right to a speedy and public trial by jury

3. The right to be represented by competent and effective counsel

4. The right to confront and cross-examine all witnesses called to testify the defendant

5. The right to produce any evidence including attendance of witnesses in the defendant's favor, and to use the subpoena power of the court to accomplish this right

6. The right to appeal any decision in a case to a higher court.

"Of all the rights enjoyed by a criminal defendant, the right to be found guilty upon proof beyond a reasonable doubt is undoubtedly one of the most important. The right ensures that our criminal justice system separates those who are guilty from those who are innocent." (note 24)

Proof beyond a reasonable doubt is the standard used by juries in criminal cases in the American, Canadian, Australian, and British legal systems to test whether the prosecution or government has met its burden of proof, and is thereby entitled to win a conviction of the defendant. The term "reasonable doubt" or "proof beyond a reasonable doubt" has been around and used for such a long period of time that it has become a part of our history and legal traditions. Many people think it needs no explanation because it is so much an integral part of our criminal justice system. In the American courts, this burden of proof or standard is a quite different standard from those used in most civil cases, which is "preponderance of the evidence".(note 25) There are two other standards called "clear and convincing evidence"(note 26), and clear, unequivocal, and convincing evidence.(note 27) The criminal standard of "proof beyond a reasonable doubt"(note 28) is a significantly higher burden than all those used in civil proceedings. And while courts do not attempt to put a quantitative value on the criminal standard, one judge has suggested that the value for the criminal standard of "beyond a reasonable doubt" would be 95% or above.(note 29) What is "reasonable doubt" and what does "proof beyond a reasonable doubt" mean? When did the "proof beyond a reasonable doubt" standard enter into the American criminal justice system? When did this standard become acknowledged as part of the basic Constitutional rights under both the 6th Amendment and the due process requirements of the 14th Amendment to the United States Constitution? To answer each of these questions, a brief history lesson is in order.

A BRIEF HISTORY OF THE "PROOF BEYOND A REASONABLE DOUBT" STANDARD

Trial by jury did not appear on the scene until the reign of Henry III. Before that time the jury was essentially a body of witnesses, called for their knowledge of the case. Judges often borrowed heavily from both their own religious and philosophical upbringings. Our present day law of evidence also began to emerge in the early 18th century. And it was during this same century that the jury emerged as a safeguard for those charged with a criminal offense. The early common law gave no guidance to judges for use by juries in criminal cases. Judges in the 16th, 17th, and 18th centuries had very little guidance and faced a very difficult task of explaining to juries what standards they should use in judging evidence.

The beyond reasonable doubt standard or doctrine evolved

as judges found it necessary to inform jurors that they must evaluate the testimony of witnesses. The right to trial by jury was universally accepted by the time of the drafting of the United States Constitution and the Bill of Rights.

THE "SATISIFIED CONSCIENCE STANDARD"

Prior to the 18th century courts used a standard called the "satisfied conscience" test.(note 30) The "satisfied conscience" standard became the first vessel into which were poured the new criteria for evaluating facts and testimony. Satisfied conscience gradually became synonymous with rational belief, that is, belief beyond reasonable doubt. A number of similar sounding phrases began to appear repeatedly in judicial charges and instructions. The first was "if you believe," the second, "if you are satisfied or not satisfied with the evidence" and a third was "satisfied conscience". Barbara J. Shapiro traced the development of early juries from its origin in the law of modern England and early Roman canon law.(note 31)

Shapiro suggests the reasonable doubt phrase was designed to help juries screen out cases. The reasonable doubt phrase first appeared in a 1752 case. There is some confusion as to whether it was first used by the prosecution or the defense, and whether it actually increased or lessened the government's burden.(note 32) However, there is no doubt that from that point on it began to be used unceasingly.

Anthony Morano says it was first used in the Boston Massacre trials of 1770, rather than in the turn of the century Irish treason trials. It was also first used in the 1796 in the Canadian legal system. In that case the jury was informed that if they had any reasonable doubt then they must acquit, "for it is the invariable direction of our English Courts of Justice to lean on the side of mercy."(note 33)

Shapiro concludes that the old concepts of probability, degrees of certainty, and moral certainty were all poured into the old formulas, and what finally emerged at the end of the eighteenth century was the moral standard of proof beyond a reasonable doubt. "The earliest standards we have identified were "satisfied belief" and "satisfied conscience." They were succeeded by "satisfied mind, or "satisfied understanding," or something closely approximating them. Gradually this language was dropped and replaced by the concept of moral certainty and proof beyond reasonable doubt.(note 34) Reasonable doubt was simply a better explanation of the satisfied conscience standard that resulted from increasing familiarity with the moral certainty concept.

In fact "reasonable doubt" was used in 1850 by the Massachusetts Supreme Judicial Court and Chief Justice Shaw in the case of *Commonwealth v. Webster*, 59 Mass. 295, 320 (1850).(note 35) That definition was later cited as one of the most satisfactory definitions ever given to the words reasonable doubt. Many state legislatures adopted it as the bases for their charges and instructions on reasonable doubt. Here is the text of that instruction:

> "[W]hat is reasonable doubt? It is a term often used, probably pretty well understood, but not easily defined. It is not mere possible doubt; because every thing relating to human affairs, and depending on moral evidence, is open to some possible or imaginary doubt. It is that state of the case, which, after the entire comparison and consideration of all the evidence, leaves the minds of jurors in that condition that they cannot say they feel an abiding conviction, to a moral certainty, of the truth of the charge. The burden of proof is upon the prosecutor. All the presumptions of law independent of evidence are in favor of innocence; and every person is presumed to be innocent until he is proved guilty. If upon such proof there is reasonable doubt remaining, the accused is entitled to the benefit of it by an acquittal. For it is not sufficient to establish a probability, though a strong one, arising from the doctrine of chances, that the fact charged is more likely to be true than the contrary; but the evidence must establish the truth of the fact to a reasonable and moral certainty; a certainty that convinces and directs the understanding, and satisfies the reason and judgment, of those who are bound to act conscientiously upon it. This we take to be proof beyond reasonable doubt.

Even though the reasonable doubt standard began to be used in both England and American law in the middle 1800's, the United States Supreme Court only recently acknowledged it as a constitutional safeguard and a fundamental part of the due process protection afforded to every criminal defendant.

"REASONABLE DOUBT STANDARD" CERTIFIED AS A REQUIREMENT OF DUE PROCESS"

It has been suggested by one writer that American courts began applying the reasonable doubt standard almost 200 years ago.(note 36) However, only recently did the United States Supreme Court certify the reasonable doubt standard as a requirement of due process of law. In 1970 in a landmark opinion, Justice Brennan wrote that the case of *In Re Winship* (note 37) presented the single and narrow question of whether proof beyond a reasonable doubt was among the essentials of due process and fair treatment required during the adjudicatory stage when a juvenile is charged with an act which would constitute a crime if committed by an adult.

Justice Brennan traced the requirement of proof beyond a reasonable doubt to the early years of the nation, beginning as early as 1798. He listed a long line of cases and suggested that the real purpose for the rule is to "safeguard men from dubious and unjust convictions with resulting forfeitures of life, liberty and property." Justice Brennan then gave additional reasons for use of the standard of proof beyond a reasonable doubt.

"The requirement of proof beyond a reasonable doubt has this vital role in our criminal procedure for cogent reasons. The accused during a criminal prosecution has at stake interest of immense importance, both because of the possibility that he may lose his liberty upon conviction and because of the certainty that he would be stigmatized by the conviction. Accordingly, a society [397 U.S. 358,364] that values the good name and freedom of every individual should not condemn a man for commission of a crime when there is reasonable doubt about his guilt."

The Court then looked at one of its earlier cases and went on to say:

As we said in Speiser v. Randall, supra, 357 U.S., at 525-526: 'There is always in litigation a margin of error, representing error in fact-finding, which both parties must take into account. Where one party has at stake an interest of transcending value-as a criminal defendant his liberty-this margin of error is reduced as to him by the process of placing on the other party the burden of ... persuading the fact finder at the conclusion of the trial of his guilt beyond a reasonable doubt. Due process commands that no man shall lose his liberty unless the Government has borne the burden of convincing the fact finder of his guilt. To this end the reasonable doubt standard is indispensable for it impresses on the trier of fact the necessity of needing a subjective state of certitude of the facts in issue."

Thus the Court specifically held "that the Due Process Clause protects the accused against conviction except upon proof beyond a reasonable doubt of every fact necessary to constitute the crime with which he is charged." [397 U.S. 358, 365].

The Court later held in *Cage v. Louisiana* 498 U.S. 39 (1990) that any jury instruction contrary to the "beyond a reasonable doubt" standard articulated in *Winship* will be considered as unconstitutional. Petitioner was convicted in a Louisiana trial court of first-degree murder, and was sentenced to death. He appealed to the Supreme Court of Louisiana, arguing, inter alia, that the reasonable doubt instruction used in the guilt phase of his trial was constitutionally defective. The instruction used in the *Cage* case was:

> *"If you entertain a reasonable doubt as to any fact or element necessary to constitute the defendant's guilt, it is your duty to give him the benefit of that doubt and return a verdict of not guilty. Even where the evidence demonstrates a probability of guilt, if it does not establish such guilt beyond a reasonable doubt, you must acquit the accused. This doubt, however, must be a reasonable one; that is one that is founded upon a real tangible substantial basis and not upon mere caprice and conjecture. It must be such doubt as would give rise to a grave uncertainty, raised in your mind by reasons of the unsatisfactory character of the evidence or lack thereof. A reasonable doubt is not a mere possible doubt. It is an actual substantial doubt. It is a doubt that a reasonable man can seriously entertain. What is required is not an absolute or mathematical certainty, but a moral certainty."* 554 So.2d 39, 41 (La. 1989) (emphasis added).

A later case said that a constitutionally deficient reasonable doubt instruction cannot be considered as harmless error. See *Sullivan v. Louisiana*, 508 U.S. 275 (1993). The instruction in the *Sullivan* case was virtually identical to the one in the *Cage* case.

There are many cases, books, articles, and treatises which suggest that the concept of reasonable doubt is often misunderstood by judges, lawyers, and laypersons. Even many of the federal circuits say that "reasonable doubt" is a fundamental concept that does not lend itself to easy refinement or definition.

There is no constitutional requirement to define reasonable doubt to a jury. The United States Supreme Court has never required trial courts to define the term. In its most recent case addressing reasonable doubt, the Court stated that the Constitution neither prohibits trial courts from defining reasonable doubt, nor requires them to do so as a matter of course. Indeed, so long as the court instructs the jury on the necessity that the defendant's guilt be proved beyond a reasonable doubt, the Constitution does not require that any particular form of words be used in advising the jury of the government's burden of proof. See, *Victor v. Nebraska*, 511 U.S. 1, 5 (1994) (citations omitted).

The 1st Circuit has joined other circuits in advising that the meaning of reasonable doubt be left to the jury to discern. The 2nd Circuit has held that a jury instruction describing the reasonable doubt standard and the presumption of innocence as rules meant "to protect the innocent and not the guilty" is reversible error.(note 38)

The 6th Circuit decisions reviewing federal criminal convictions have explicitly discouraged or condemned instructions defining reasonable doubt, as other circuits have done. Instead, 6th Circuit decisions have said that if some definition should be given, the only real question is what the definition should say.(note 39) The 7th Circuit recommends that no instruction be given defining reasonable doubt, and has said, "The Court has found that an attempt to define reasonable doubt presents a risk without any real benefit." The Court even suggests that the term should not be defined even if the jury asks it to do so during deliberations. The term is self-explanatory and is its own best definition.

Both federal and state Courts have been presented with numerous attempts to define reasonable doubt. All such definitions have in some way attempted to elaborate, explain, or define the phrase.(note 40) The majority of these attempts at definition have been rejected by the courts. They have included "substantial doubt" "honest doubt" "fair doubt" "grave uncertainty" "actual substantial doubt" and "moral certainty."

Many criminal defense lawyers continue to ask that Courts not define "reasonable doubt" because all such definitions tend to be pro-prosecution. Chief Justice Wilkinson, in his dissent in *Walton* says that a picture is often worth a thousand words, and sometimes the fewer the words the better. "So it is with "reasonable doubt. The majesty of the word has always been its brevity. It is not at all a bad thing for a jury to be left to work through its meaning."(note 41) "The problem with "reasonable doubt" however, is that juries do not necessarily know it when they see it, because both legislatures and the Courts have been unwilling to tell them what it is, beyond a few unhelpful clichés. Courts are quite willing to tell juries what reasonable doubt is not."(note 42)

The 1806 Kentucky revision of the criminal law not only began with a treatment of evidence in criminal prosecutions, but also discusses the several degrees of evidence and certainty in history, natural history, astronomy, and law. It also contained the beyond reasonable doubt language.(note 43)

In Kentucky prosecutors, defense lawyers, and the Courts are now prohibited from defining reasonable doubt based on *Commonwealth v. Callahan*, 675 S.W. 2d 391 (1984). However, and as a result of *Taylor v. Kentucky*, 436 U.S. 478, 98 S.Ct. 1930, L.Ed. 2d 468 (1978), the United Supreme Court held it as reversible error not to instruct on the presumption of innocence and reasonable doubt when requested to do so by the defendant.

As a result of that case, the Instruction in Kentucky was

rewritten, and is now called the Presumption of Innocence Instruction, and is required to be given in every case by the Kentucky Criminal Rules. (note 44) In every criminal case the jury shall be instructed substantially as follows:

The law presumes a defendant to be innocent of a crime and the indictment shall not be considered as evidence or as having any weight against him. You shall find the defendant not guilty unless you are satisfied from the evidence alone and beyond a reasonable doubt that he or she is guilty. If upon the whole case you have reasonable doubt that he or she is guilty, you shall find him or her not guilty.

How does a criminal defense attorney undertake the difficult task of incorporating these two fundamental legal principles into an overall trial strategy, and hopefully a strategy that will contribute to the jury returning a not guilty verdict?

It is the attorney's responsibility to insure that the jury does not forget about the presumption of innocence and has at least a basic understanding of both the "presumption of innocence" and the burden of proof "beyond a reasonable doubt" standard used in a criminal case. Since juries are required to deliberate rationally, and cannot just go to the jury room and toss a coin, [as one recent jury did in a Kentucky criminal case] jurors cannot possibly undertake this solemn task and be true to their oath if they do not understand the concept, and know how to go about applying it to the facts and evidence and the Instructions of law as given to them by the Court.

I will cite twelve ways in which I believe the above task can be accomplished.

TWELVE WAYS TO USE THE "PROOF BEYOND A REASONABLE DOUBT"

1. Explain and fully press for an understanding by the jury of both fundamental and basic principles. The government has the entire burden. The burden stays with government and never shifts to the defendant, and the defendant is not required to prove his or her innocence. The defendant is not required to produce any evidence at all, or to challenge any of the government's evidence. The defendant is not required to call any witnesses, or cross examine any of the government's witnesses.

2. Give the reasons and purposes for the reasonable doubt standard. This standard can be defined by comparing it to the other

types or standards of proof, and that it is substantially higher than the other three standards of proof used in civil cases.

3. Show that under our system of justice it is much better if one, ten, or fifty, (whatever number he chooses to use) guilty go free, than one innocent person be convicted.

4. Convince and persuade the jurors that its definition of reasonable doubt must come from their common understanding, and from the inferences and analogies given to them by the defense attorney during the trial, and in his or her closing arguments.

5. Don't wait or count on the court or the government's attorneys to mention either principle as part of their trial strategy. The government's attorneys hardly ever mention it. As an attorney, do not be afraid to understand, grasp, and be capable of fully defining in laymen's terms the "presumption of innocence" and "proof beyond a reasonable doubt" for the jury. Even though the court says that you cannot define reasonable doubt, there are many ways to explain and impart the meaning, and still comply with the rule.

6. Point out to the jury areas in the evidence from which they can find reasonable doubts.

7. List for the jury reasonable doubts that you have found in the evidence and from the record.

8. Ask the jurors to share their reasonable doubts with their fellow jurors.

9. Suggest key points and areas in the evidence that raise not only doubt, but uncertainty, speculation, probabilities, possibilities, guesswork, inferences, hunches, mistaken beliefs, and "reasonable doubt." Make reasonable inferences and show that those inferences lead to reasonable doubt.

10. Show that the scales of justice actually come down on the side of your client's innocence rather than his or her guilt.

11. Use language and opinions from court cases to sum up and explain reasonable doubt. Here is one that could well be used by an attorney.

"In the end, only a jury can truly define reasonable doubt. Reasonable

doubt cannot be divorced from its specific context any more than the concepts of "reason" or a "reasonable person." Jurors differ in their own individual conceptions of reasonable doubt. During jury deliberations, these jurors debate whether or not the prosecution in the specific case before them has proven the guilt of a particular defendant beyond a reasonable doubt." (See Note 45)

    12. Emphasize these principles throughout the entire trial, during the jury selection, in opening statements, in the instructions, and finally in the closing argument. Read the Instruction on reasonable doubt to the jury. And finally blow it up on a chart for the jury to look at and so they can read it while you are closing. Also, don't forget to use reasonable doubt in your defense of juveniles and in juvenile court cases.

    Always remember "proof beyond a reasonable doubt and the "presumption of innocence." As a criminal defense attorney, don't ever forget them, and don't try to defend a client or go to trial without them!

Twelve Pointers to
Not Guilty Every Time

1. **Always thank the jury**
   A. Be gracious to them and they will reward you
   B. Explain and comment on why the jury system is the best

2. **Remind jurors of their commitments**
   A. Remind jurors of commitments as to indictment not being evidence,
   B. Who has the burden, and who has no burden
   C. Fairly and impartially decide case on evidence and Instructions of law
   D. Caution jurors that a not guilty verdict is following the law
   E. Defendant not testifying and reasonable doubt

3. **Remind jurors of promises made by you and kept**
   A. Promised no more than you can deliver
   B. Deliver all that you promised
   C. Admit or stipulate to what you have to and what is against you

4. **Hold prosecutors accountable for promises made and broken**
   A. If witnesses were promised and not delivered, question why?
   B. If evidence was promised and not delivered, question why?
   C. If case has gaping holes, point them out

5. **Ask jury to set aside sympathy or prejudices**
   A. Sympathize with a victim of violence or abuse
   B. Show the jury they can empathize with the victim and still find the defendant not guilty

6. **Weave the Instructions with the Facts**
   A. Show the jury that the judge gave you what you asked for and how the Instructions favor you

6. Always read the Reasonable Doubt Instruction or chart it
    C. Blow up the instruction on Reasonable Doubt for the jury to read.

7. **Test your defendant's guilt from the evidence**
    A. Go through key evidence and show it favors your client
    B. Show the jury you believe deeply in your client's case and his innocence from the evidence
    C. Use prosecutors own words to make your case
    D. Be confident and able to convince the jury that your side is the right side

8. **Dissect only key witness testimony**
    A. Boil case down to 1-3 witnesses and no more
    B. If you haven't been hurt, give witness no attention
    C. If a witness has been honest, but is mistaken point out both

9. **Reasonable Doubt, Reasonable Doubt, Reasonable Doubt!***
    A. Show jurors areas where they can find reasonable doubt
    B. Give a little history of the purpose of presumption of innocence and the rule on reasonable doubt
    C. Ask jurors to share their reasonable doubts with fellow jurors
    D. Always read the reasonable doubt instruction
    E. Use the 12 Pointers for Reasonable Doubt in Chapter 4 of this book

10. **Appeal to jury's sense of fairness and justice**
    A. If police have done a sloppy or incomplete investigation, say so. If they have done an admirable job, commend them
    B. If case shouldn't have been brought to trial or dismissed, say so
    C. Show why a verdict would be unfair to your client and harmful to our system of justice

11. **Close the Closing with Passion and Emotion**
    A. Ask the jury to send a message by their verdict
    B. Be prepared to end early and always be ready to close

C. Keep the prosecution guessing on whether your client will testify

12. **Ask the Jury for What You Want - A Not Guilty Verdict**
    A. Remind the jury of what's at stake and to take its time
    B. To get a verdict of one or a hung jury, ask the jury to stand
    C. Thank the jury again

CASE #1

Date of verdict:	September 14, 1982
Charge:	Assault First Degree
	Class B Felony
Possible sentence:	10 to 20 years
Judge:	Hon. Charles Anderson
	Jefferson Circuit Court
Prosecutor:	Hon. Amy Garon

Defendant's closing argument:	30 minutes (estimate)
Commonwealth's closing argument:	35 minutes (estimate)
Length of jury deliberations:	unknown
Reasonable doubt used	1 time
Was defendant a convicted felon?	NO
Did defendant testify?	YES
Verdict:	**NOT GUILTY**

SYNOPSIS

The defendant was indicted on one count of Assault 1st stemming from the shooting of David Wayne Stringer in June 1982 in Louisville, Kentucky.

The defendant was called by his ex-wife to come to her apartment on the pretense that her new boyfriend had threatened to harm and kidnap their four-year old daughter. She had called her brother and her father, but neither would come to help her.

When the defendant got to her apartment, the victim arrived shortly thereafter and already had several knives in his hand. He testified that he had the knives because he was attempting to change the locks. However, the ex-wife of the defendant and the officer testified that there was nothing wrong with the locks on the door. When the victim continued to advance, the defendant shot twice. The victim lost his spleen, had several fractured ribs, and stayed in the hospital fifty five days.

After the defendant shot the victim, he walked to the Hardee's Restaurant nearby, and sat down, and asked the manager to call the police, and tell them he had just shot a man. The defendant took the stand and testified at trial. The judge instructed the jury on Assault 1st and the lesser included offense of Assault 2nd. After deliberations, the Jury found the defendant **NOT GUILTY** of Assault 1st and **NOT GUILTY** of Assault 2nd.

CLOSING ARGUMENT

May it please the Court, ladies and gentlemen of the jury. First of all, I would like to express my appreciation and thanks on behalf of myself and my client and his family for the attention that you have paid during this trial, the attentiveness to which you have listened to all of the evidence and to all of the witnesses. We thank you for that.

I ask you to bear with me just a moment while I attempt to draw together for you the facts, and present them to you so that you can make a proper decision. That is the purpose of our final argument. You understand that under our judicial system, the prosecutor gets the last word. You also understand that just as the judge has instructed, her last words, just as my last words, are not evidence. So it is very important that you listen to what I say, because after I set down I cannot get up again and refute whatever she might say.

When each of you were questioned during the Voir Dire, the examination at the beginning of this trial, we asked you several things. First, we asked you if you understood that the indictment, the piece of paper by which this case was brought into Court, was not evidence against the defendant and you said you understood that.

We also asked you whether you understood that the defendant was presumed innocent at the beginning of the trial and all during the trial. It is only after you reach your verdict that the presumption goes away. We also asked you whether you understood that the defendant did not have to say anything, or did not have to take the stand and testify. And that the Commonwealth through its prosecutor, Ms. Garon, has the burden of proving that the defendant is guilty of assault and that it must prove his guilt beyond a reasonable doubt.

You said you understood that and we believed you. You further indicated that you understood and we believed you that if the evidence justified an acquittal, or if the evidence justified a verdict of not guilty, that in so determining that verdict, if the evidence warranted it, that you would also be following the law.

And finally you said that you understood that if the court instructed you regarding self-defense or self protection, and which it has, that you would follow that law, even though you disagreed with that law, or thought it should be different.

You have now been instructed as to the law in this case. I would like to go through, not each Instruction, but go through and point out to you Instruction #1, Assault 1st and Instruction #2, Assault 2nd degree. The only difference between Instruction # 1 and Instruction #2, Assault 1st and Assault 2nd, is that in order for you to find him guilty of Assault in the First Degree, you have to find that David Wayne Stringer sustained a serious physical injury. If you find that he did not sustain a serious physical injury, and find that the defendant shot him intentionally, and that he did not do so in self-defense, then you must find him guilty under Instruction #2.

Ladies and gentlemen from the very beginning of this case, we indicated to you what our proof would be. We indicated to you what we would admit. We admitted that the defendant shot David Wayne Stringer, that he did so with that gun and that he didn't deny it. He has never denied it. David Wayne Stringer took the stand. You saw him tell you about his injuries. You will have to judge between that. He was seriously hurt. So really in my mind, and I believe that if you look at the evidence, there is no question about him being seriously hurt, the only question is whether he was shot as a result of attempting to inflict serious bodily harm, or possibly death upon the defendant.

You will also note in Instruction #3, regarding self protection, that at the time the defendant shot David Wayne Stringer, as mentioned in Instruction #1 and in Instruction #2, he believed that David Wayne Stringer was then and there about to use physical force upon him, he was privileged to use such physical force against David Wayne Stringer as he believed necessary in order to protect himself from him, but including the right to use deadly physical force in so doing, only if he believed it was necessary in order to protect himself from death or serious physical injury at the hands of David Wayne Stringer.

Now you have heard all of the witnesses testify, and we have stipulated that the gun and those knives are both deadly weapons. You have heard the officer testify that those weapons could kill or could seriously hurt someone. There is no question that those are deadly weapons and we won't deny that those are deadly weapons.

However, right under self-protection, there will be a definition of physical force. Now I want you to look at that because that's the key. Physical force means force used upon or directed towards. Force used upon.... and we didn't say any force was used upon him, but he certainly was provoked. The knives were upon him. You have heard the defendant testify that David kept coming at him, and he told him, "Man don't keep walking up on me with those knives." Physical force means force used upon or directed toward the body of another person.

We trusted you at the beginning of this case, and we trust you now, and we know that you will uphold the Oath to which you swore that you would listen patiently to all of the evidence, and without prejudice or sympathy for the defendant or prejudice or sympathy for David Stringer, even though he had been in the hospital for fifty five days. It's natural for us to have sympathy toward the injuries he sustained but that sympathy must not influence your verdict.

Ladies and gentlemen of the jury there is not much in dispute here. That the defendant shot David Stringer, as charged in the indictment, he does not deny. But he asserts that he did not do so voluntarily or with malice, that he committed the act from necessity, from the prompting instinct of nature, self defense. I believed that Ms. Garon asked him the question, "Was it his instinct that caused him to take that gun out there"? And I believe he said yes. That is the oldest and most universal law of nature, the right of self defense. He denies that he either violated the law of God or the law of man. He was merely defending himself and defending his own life.

He asserts and I shall attempt to show you and confirm to you from the evidence that David Stringer intended to inflict serious bodily harm, and or death upon the defendant.

Now he has indicated to you in his testimony that he had those knives because he was attempting to change the lock on the door. Now ladies and gentlemen, you have to judge for yourselves whether those are the kinds of tools that someone would use to fix a lock. What his common law wife said, as Ms. Garon calls her, or his girlfriend, she indicated to you that there was nothing wrong with the locks on the door. Officer Blaser testified that he didn't see anything wrong with the lock on the door. And she even testified as to the backdoor, that the refrigerator was in front of the door.

Ladies and gentlemen it is pretty obvious why he went back into the kitchen. And when he came out, he indicated to you he went back in the kitchen, and when he came out he had those two knives.

Secondly, I would submit that even though the defendant received no cuts, he didn't even receive a scratch, he didn't receive any wounds, yet he had reasonable grounds to believe that David Wayne Stringer would injure him with the two knives that he had in his hands as close as he was to him. And there has been a little controversy as to whether he was four feet, or five feet, or six feet. It doesn't make much difference because I believe you heard him testify that David was close enough, that if he even raised the knife, he could have cut him. The defendant was justified in what he did because he did it for the protection of his own life, just as if he had been cut or stabbed with those knives.

The law of these two points is very simple and is nothing more than the universal law of nature. Nature has endowed every species of living creature with the instinct of self preservation. That a man has an absolute right to defend himself from great bodily harm and to resist an attempt to inflict upon him personal violence, personal danger, even to the death of his assailant, I presume cannot be disputed.

The defendant took defensive action proportionate to the apparent and the impending violence and sufficient to prevent it. You heard the defendant testify that he only shot twice. David wants us to believe that he shot him three, four, or five times. You heard the officer testify that the doctor may have indicated that some of those were exit wounds and some were entry wounds. And there has been nothing to dispute Robert's testimony that he only shot David twice.

You have also heard David testify that he shot him first, and then fell to his knees, and as he was on his knees, he shot him again. But that is totally contradictory from what Janice said. That is totally contradictory from what the defendant said, and it is totally contradictory from what the defendant said in his statement.

In his statement he said, "He shot me, and as I was turning to walk away, he shot me again. Now ladies and gentlemen you've got three different situations. First, we have him being shot the first time and him falling to his knees. Then we have him being shot and him turning away. Then we have him being shot, and him walking away, and then he is shot again. You have to judge the evidence as it came from the witnesses who took the stand.

Let's proceed to test the innocence or the guilt of the defendant by the evidence that's been presented. As indicated during Ms. Garon's opening, this case comes down to about three witnesses; the defendant, David Stringer, and Janice Combs. And the defendant admitted, and I admitted in my opening, everything that the prosecutor has brought out; that he shot him, that it is a deadly weapon, that he turned himself in, and that he showed the police where the weapon was. The Commonwealth put on numerous witnesses, of course, trying to make a case where there is no case.

They put on four or five officers. What did those officers tell us? They were not present. They don't know what started it, and why it happened. All they know is that they were called to the scene of a shooting. Shortly thereafter, another call came in from Hardee's Restaurant, that the defendant was there, and that he wanted to give himself up and that he did so. And then he showed the Officers where the gun was, and he then went with Detective Maupin and made a voluntary statement.

They didn't prove or add to anything that I did not tell you in my Opening Statement from those police witnesses. So, the testimony and the evidence in this case comes down to three witnesses. But all of these police officers, every single one of them, testified that the defendant was very cooperative. He gave them no problems, and that he showed them where the weapon was.

The Commonwealth's first witness, and of course the most important witness, because he is the victim, is David Stringer. And what did he say that was different from what the defendant said, and from what Janice said? And I just want to go over a few of the things he said, because you heard the evidence and I am sure that you remember the evidence.

First, he said that the defendant put a gun to his head, and said, "bang, bang, if you do anything to my wife or my child I will kill you." You heard Janice testify that she was right in the room, and that the defendant never said that. And David said that Shauntay was nowhere around. You heard Janice testify that Shauntay was there. In fact, you heard the defendant testify that at one point he told Shauntay, "get out of the way."

At that point David pulled the knives out of his pocket, and she ran behind him. And that in going back to that corner, that he stepped on her foot and almost stumbled over her, and it was at that point that he couldn't back up any further.

And you also heard David Stringer testify that he had the knives for putting the locks on the door, but you heard Janice testify that there was nothing wrong with the locks, and that if David said that he was lying. You also heard her testify that she had sworn out two warrants for Mr. Stringer and that of those warrants, the first warrant indicated that he broke up all of her furniture and threw away all of her clothes, and that the estimated value of those clothes was $300.00

But you heard him testify that he never bothered anything that belonged to her, that the only things that he threw away belonged to him. You also heard her testify that she told the people at the warrant desk, and its right there, you can take it back to the jury room with you, that he tried to smother her with the pillow. He says that he didn't try to smother her with the pillow. She also said that he put a rifle to her head, and told her he could kill her, but she only told the people at the warrant desk that so they could do something about it.

And you heard her testify that her brother wouldn't come to help her. Her father wouldn't come to help her. She called the police and the police wouldn't come to help her. She swore under oath to that warrant, and swore that everything in that warrant was true, and she signed her name to it. You have to judge that evidence and the credibility of that witness for yourself.

You have also heard her state that she was at her mother's house, and David came by there, and told her that he had moved all of his things out. However, he says in his testimony, "that he had not moved all his suits out, and that if she wanted to keep her things, she had better go get them or they could be stolen.

Ladies and gentlemen of the jury, I believe that David knew at that point when he told her that she should go back there to get those things, that she would probably have her husband accompany her to get those things. And that is why he told her, and that is why he doubled back, and went back there, and came in immediately after they got there. It wasn't an hour or two later. It was right after they got there.

You heard the defendant testify and you heard Janice testify, that when he went in he slammed the door, and he slammed it so hard that the door didn't even close, it just came back open. And David indicated in his testimony, that he has got a real high temper. And all of the evidence in this case that has been presented from that witness stand is to the effect that David is violent, has a high temper, and he's an angry person.

He's a person who beat up Janice numerous times, he's a person who destroyed furniture, not only that weekend, but he destroyed furniture at the home of Janice's mother. Mrs. Williams took the stand and told you about that.

David's actions were violent on Friday and on Saturday. They were so violent and so bad that she came down and swore out a warrant for him. They were so violent and so bad that she called her brother. He wouldn't help her. She called her father and he wouldn't help her. So she finally decided to call her husband and tell him that her daughter had been kidnapped. And knowing his love for his daughter, Lameeka who is four years old, she knew that he would respond and go with her to that apartment.

And what's her motive? We have to look to her motive. Of course, she knows that her marriage between her and the defendant is over. He indicated to you that he was going to get a divorce as soon as this is over. But she knew that if she wants to hang on with David Stringer, that she better say something to bolster her side of the story.

Now the second witness, Janice Combs, took the stand. You heard her testify, totally different, totally contradictory, from what David had said as to the fact that the defendant put a gun to his head. And as to the fact that David went in the kitchen, and when he came back she noticed two knives, and that he had them in both hands.

The most important thing in the statement, the first statement that she gave, a couple of hours after this incident, the detective asked her, "Did David Wayne Stringer ever remove the knives from his back pocket"? And her answer was no. Twenty four hours, later she goes back to the police department, and makes an additional statement, and says she forgot a few things.

Ladies and gentlemen, it is obvious she didn't forget. She wanted to change her story to tell the truth. And she knows she would probably be caught in a lie. My great-grandmother used to tell me something that I have found to be true to this very day, and that is that a liar is worse than a thief. A thief usually gets caught the first or second time around, but a liar keeps on going. But eventually a liar just gets wound up in his own mess.

And that is what happened to Janice Combs in this case. She deliberately changed her statements because the question was asked, "Did he ever remove the knives from his back pocket"? And she said no. And to clarify it and reaffirm it, Detective Maupin reiterated, he did not. Yet twenty four hours later, she goes back and makes a totally different statement.

Again, you have to judge her credibility. Another thing that she didn't say is that she never went back and changed the warrants, or told them it was not true. Everything is true, except for the area about the weapons, which is the most critical and most important area.

The Commonwealth suggests that you tell the defendant that he must go to the penitentiary for ten to twenty years because he wanted to defend himself. The law of self defense has always been construed more liberally in our country than in any other country, because we have more to protect, we have more to defend.

It is the apprehension of harm to you and danger, and not the actual existence which justifies self-defense. Why should he wait? What did he have to wait until? Did he have to wait until the knives were in his heart and in his chest? Did he have to wait until David had already inflicted serious harm before he could defend himself? No.

Just as if our country were attacked tonight by a foreign foe, we wouldn't wait until our cities were burning and our countryside was laid to waste by bombs. We would send forth armies, and we would send forth men to defend ourselves. Just as a hunter is in the jungle, and if a tiger springs out, you shoot him the moment you see him.

But the Commonwealth wants you to send this defendant to the penitentiary on the evidence that has come from that witness stand, and I believe that would be a travesty of justice to do so.

Had the defendant given David Stringer one more second, one more inch to come just a little closer, we might have a different defendant on trial. We might have a different victim sitting here, and we might have a different defense.

The defendant's only intent was to stop David Wayne Stringer and that is what he did. And by your verdict of not guilty, you will be saying to this defendant that what he did was in self defense. And you will be saying to David Wayne Stringer, that we don't live by the law of the jungle. We live by the laws by which all of us are governed, and which are for our own protection.

And that if a man threatens your life, you don't have to wait until the threat is carried out, you are privileged to act in self defense. It is only when you believe it is everlasting too late. The defendant told you he only pulled it at the last minute, when he was backed up in the corner with his daughter behind him. You have to ask yourselves what was going through his mind at that time.

Ladies and gentlemen, I know that you will return a verdict of not guilty as to all of these charges. Thank You!

CASE #2

Date of verdict:	May 11, 1988
Charges:	Sodomy First Degree Class A Felony (victim under 12)
Possible sentence:	20 to 50 years or Life
Judge:	Hon. Olga Peers, Jefferson Circuit Court
Prosecutor:	Hon. Kelly Miller
Defendants opening argument:	8 minutes
Defendants closing argument:	23 minutes
Commonwealth's closing argument:	30 minutes
Reasonable Doubt used	16 times
Length of jury deliberations:	7 hours, 22 minutes
Was defendant a convicted felon?	NO
Did defendant testify?	YES
Verdict:	**HUNG JURY***

* **Commonwealth elected not to retry the defendant and an Alford plea was entered on a misdemeanor charge with no time to serve and court costs**

SYNOPSIS

The defendant was indicted on the charge of Sodomy in the 1st degree for alleged acts of sexual abuse on a six year old girl that occurred between May 12, 1985 and June 15, 1985 in Louisville, Jefferson County, Kentucky. The child was the daughter of his ex-girlfriend and was nine at the time of the trial.

A co-defendant, a firefighter, was indicted for the exact same charges for the same period of time. Both the victim and the co-defendant testified, along with both mothers and the child's maternal grandmother.

The trial began in May 1988 and took several days. At the end of the trial, the jury was instructed on the single count of Sodomy in the 1st degree. After jury deliberations began, the jury requested and was allowed to rehear 40 minutes of testimony. They retired for the night without reaching a verdict.

The next morning the jury returned and asked to rehear all of the testimony. The judge refused and sent them back for continued deliberations. After another two hours, the jury returned to court and was read the Allen charge. After another couple of hours, the jury returned and said they were hopelessly deadlocked **(hung jury)**.* The court declared a mistrial.

The case was finally settled on an Alford plea with the defendant pleading to a misdemeanor and receiving 12 months conditionally discharged for 2 years and court costs of $47.50.

*A hung jury means that the jury after lengthy deliberations cannot unanimously decide upon guilt or innocence forcing the judge to declare a mistrial. A mistrial in this case means the termination of the trial because of the deadlock by the jury.

OPENING ARGUMENT

Judge Peers, Ms. Miller, ladies and gentlemen of the jury. It is customary at this time for counsel to talk to you about the case, and to indicate what the evidence will show, and hopefully this will help you to follow the evidence as it comes in and put it in its proper place.

What I say to you should serve to give you a general outline of what the evidence will show. This is a most serious allegation. I would be less than fair and honest with you if I said that sexual assaults and sexual crimes don't occur. They occur to both men and women and to both adults and children. And all of us are community and civic and responsibly minded enough that we don't want people who commit these crimes to be around our children or to be around us. And the law allows for punishment of these crimes.

Ladies and gentlemen, the evidence is so weak and it is so clear that there is no evidence in this case, that it is hard to believe that this case is before you today. Ms. Miller read to you a part of the indictment, count one charging that between May 12, 1985... And I ask you to keep that date in mind, because the testimony will show beyond a reasonable doubt, that this gentlemen who is in the United States Army, he did not even get back into the country, and did not get back into Louisville until May 16th. And she failed to read to you count two of the indictment in which this defendant was also charged with rape. [*Objection by Commonwealth-sustained by Court since rape charge had been dismissed*]

The evidence will be such that some two years after this incident we have a report allegedly to a grandmother that two people molested this child and both charged with the same thing. The child was taken to the hospital and examined. There were no signs of any trauma. There were no abrasions. There were no tears. There were no scars. The child never complained of any itching or burning. No one ever noticed any unusual smells or unusual discharges, any unusual odors. There was no discoloration or no discomfort, either in February of 1985 or two years earlier. Cultures were taken of the child both of her vagina, of her rectum, and her throat. All of these cultures came back negative. Negative for everything; negative for gonorrhea, negative for syphilis and negative for chlamydia. There was no evidence of sodomy because no sodomy took place by this defendant who is on trial for his life.

The defendant will get on the stand and tell you he had a relationship with this woman, just like another witness, Arthur Lewis

White, will tell you he had a relationship with this woman. In fact there is evidence and the evidence will come out that this lady had numerous relationships all at the same time. But for some reason this child makes an allegation that someone has touched her. The evidence will show that this woman had numerous relationships with numerous men all around the same time and at the same time. The evidence will also show that she was in love with this man and obsessed with him; obsessed to the point that she wanted to marry him. And the evidence will show that he told her he did not want to marry her because of all of those relationships.

The evidence will also show clearly this man never lived with this woman. And during the time period alleged in this indictment, as I have already indicated, he was not in the country for a portion of those days. It was not a month and a half, as Ms. Miller would have you believe, it was only 29 days he was on leave and immediately upon his arrival the mother, by some mysterious reason, knew he was in town and was at his mother's house when he arrived. His evidence and the evidence will show he never lived never with this woman and never paid any utilities. He never bought any food, never bathed this child ,never fed this child, and he never clothed this child, because this is not his child.

And he did on occasions spend the night with the mother, but when he spent the night with the mother, the child was with the grandparents where she stayed most of the time. The evidence will show that the only reason he is charged with this offense is because he no longer preferred a relationship with this lady, and did not want to marry her. The evidence will also show that the mother indicates she showed pictures to the child. But she has never told anyone how many pictures, or whose pictures those were that she showed to the child, when the child picked out two people as to the ones bothering her. The evidence will show from the defendant and his mother that when he was on leave for those 29 days, that he lived with his mother. He did visit her on occasion and he did stay there, and he is not denying that at all.

But the evidence will show that no not once, never, ever, did he take indecent liberties with this child. And no, not once, never, ever, has he taken indecent liberties with any child. The evidence will show that this man has been mostly in the military or in school for most of his adult life. He has never been arrested, other than when he was arrested on this charge, and the evidence will clearly show that. The evidence will also show that no other people were ever checked out; other people that lived with this child or this mother, other people that baby-sit or bathed this child, as being possible people that messed with this child, if she was messed with. None of those people were ever checked out. Medical evidence there is none, direct evidence there is none. And now this child has talked with so many people, detectives social workers, commonwealth attorneys, she is obviously confused and mistaken as to whether anybody has touched her or whether somebody has told her to say that somebody has touched her.

And you will see that varying things have been told. First she was raped. Second it was oral sodomy. Third it was anal sodomy. Next it happened four or five times, then nine or ten time. He put his fingers inside of her. All varying stories, varying every time as to the details, and as to when it happened, and where it happened.

Ladies and gentlemen, there is not one piece of evidence here that this defendant ever sodomized this child, either orally or anally, or did anything else to this child. We will ask you at the end of this case to return a verdict of not guilty.

CLOSING ARGUMENT

May it please the Court, Honorable Judge Peers, Ms. Miller, Detective Majors, ladies and gentlemen of the jury. First of all, let me on behalf of my client say that we thank you for serving as jurors in this case. We all know that jury service and jury duty is not easy and everyone does not want to do it.

But on behalf of my client and as an Officer of the Court, I'd like to thank you for sitting these two days, listening attentively, and asking pertinent questions. And what you are about to do is most important, and that is the final act, rendering a verdict in this case.

For just a few minutes, I would like to summarize the evidence, and to present it so it will help you to make a just and proper decision in this case. When I sit down the prosecutor will have the last word, and I won't have a chance to get back up and rebut anything that she might say. So it is very important that each one of you, the twelve that are finally seated, listen to me now. It is very important.

When you were first brought into this courtroom yesterday, we asked you several things. And you said that you understood. We asked you whether you understood that the indictment was not any evidence and could not be used as evidence. You said you understood that. We asked you whether you understood that my client was presumed to be innocent of these charges until proof is put on that convinces each one of you beyond a reasonable doubt as to his guilt.

We also asked you whether you understood that the Commonwealth, represented by Kelly Miller, has the burden of proving that he is guilty. He doesn't have to prove he is innocent, but they have to prove his guilt, and prove it to each one of you twelve, beyond a reasonable doubt.

We also indicated to you and you said that you understood, and the judge told you, that he didn't have to testify; but that he would testify, but that if he didn't want to testify, that was his right. And you said you understood all of those things. And I have to mention those things, because you have to be guided by those things in your deliberations.

The presumption of innocence means that he is presumed innocent until he is proven guilty. And the indictment "has no weight" means that you can't use it in your deliberations to determine his guilt or innocence.

And we also asked you and you promised that you would look beyond any biases, any sympathies, any prejudices that you might have, whether for the child or my client, in deciding the evidence in this case. But to decide the case solely based on the evidence that came from that chair, and the Instructions of law as given to you by the Court. And I don't have to go over the Instructions with you. You can read them, but I will point out a couple of things.

[*Hagan reading Instruction No. 1*], you will find him guilty under this instruction, and I'll repeat it, if and only if you believe from the evidence beyond a reasonable doubt. And then Instruction No. 3, you shall find him guilty unless you are satisfied from the evidence alone and beyond a reasonable doubt. And if upon the whole case, you have a doubt, you shall find him not guilty. I'll ask you to look at these Instructions when you go back to the jury room.

Now all of us have to feel sympathy anytime a child is hurt, anytime a child is victimized, in fact anytime anything like these allegations happen to a child. That's natural. You feel it. I feel it. Even those of us who don't have children feel it.. We have to feel that way. That's the natural mindset of a community minded, honorable, decent citizen. But I am asking you to set aside any feelings of sympathy that you might have for this child, and to give my client the fair trial that he's entitled to, and decide this case on those two things; the evidence alone, and these Instructions of law.

And at the beginning of this case, I promised you that I would be fair with you. I gave you a promissory note. And I told you that there was no evidence here, other than what this child said, that my client did anything to this child. No medical evidence. No evidence of any other witness. No evidence of any other allegations. And I believe we kept that promise.

I ask you to look at that evidence and see first of all if it raises reasonable doubt #1 in your mind. And I don't have to retrace of any of what the witnesses said, because you heard all of them. And you can use your own fairness, your own honesty, your own common sense, to determine the credibility and the believability of all witnesses.

Now I listened and I took few notes during the prosecutors opening. They promised you several things also. First they asked you to take your life experiences and use them. You didn't have to have any particular expertise in deciding this case. Just take your own common life time experiences, and use them in judging the evidence here.

And I would point out to you reasonable doubt No. 2. The child and the detective say that this happened day and night, weekend after weekend. The detective says nine or ten times. The child says five times. Look at what the grandmother said regarding who kept the child on the weekends. She kept the child most of the time. She was not with the mother. She was with the grandmother because she wanted to go to church. Now the mother says that she kept her on the weekend. That ought to raise a doubt in your mind.

And then I asked you to take this diary back to the jury room with you and look through it. Look at all the names. Look at all the names. How many names of different people that had a relationship with or lived with Petina Asher.

And I ask you to look at May 12th. The indictment says it happened during May 12th to June 15th. My client didn't even get back in the country until the fifteenth, and didn't get back into the county until the sixteenth. But it was the mother that gave those dates.

And then look at all the different versions. She goes to see the detective. She goes to see the CHR protective services worker days apart, and tells an entirely different story. She tells the CHR worker about the incident on the couch in which he came in with the blanket, kneeled down, and told her to kneel down in front of him, and told her to lick his penis.

And then the next day, she goes in and tells an entirely different story to this officer. She tells about a finger incident that happened numerous times. She didn't tell that incident to Detective Majors. She told that incident to the social worker, Pat Davis.

And then the mother, she was adamant that she kept a diary of everybody who stayed over there, or who had contact, or came over to her house. And I ask you to look at that diary, and see on how many weekends, during May 16th to June 16th, that the defendant's name appears on the weekend. He was not even here on May 12 or May 15th, and yet for a part of the indictment, he is indicted for a crime that allegedly occurred during that time.

But the most important thing that the prosecutor said in her Opening Statement, "We will bring you evidence, living breathing proof and testimony that he sodomized this child." And I ask you ladies and gentlemen, other than the words of that child, who said she talked to so may people, she even said a thousand, and talked to them thousands of times, where is the evidence? Where is the living breathing proof and testimony? Have they kept their promise?

And on the other hand, I told you that this man's record was impeccable. And there has not been one iota of evidence that it is not. And you can believe that with all the vast resources-city police, county police, Commonwealth attorney's office, state police and the FBI-that if there was one blemish, if there was tarnish on this man's character, they would have found it and brought it in to this courtroom. They didn't find it because there is none.

And then have you heard any testimony, you heard the questions relating to beatings of the mother and child, and stealing from the mother and child? Have you heard any testimony regarding that from any witnesses? No you have not. They have not kept their promises.

And then you heard how many relationships there were. And you can look through the book, and see how many names that I gave you. Even though now, some of them are supposed to be clients, and they come over to get their hair fixed at her home, even though her business was somewhere else.

In her own words, she had many flings. Not just this last fling, when she was engaged to her present husband. But she wanted one last fling with the defendant, in her own words. And we haven't tried to shift any blame here. And I can't say if somebody has messed with this child or not. But I can tell you that there has been no proof, medical proof that anybody messed with this child, and there certainly hasn't been any proof, other than the one word of that child, that she was messed with by the defendant.

No tears, no lacerations, no unusual odors, no discharges, no venereal diseases, no chlamydia, no gonorrhea, no syphilis, nothing. And you heard the mother testify, that this child stayed at home a lot by herself. At age six, she was a latchkey child, which means she was given a key to keep herself most of the time, to let herself in and out, most of the time, a six year old child.

And then do you wonder, and does it raise another doubt in your mind as to why the mother did not show the photographs, and give the names of other people that were living with her, and with whom she had a relationship to the detective?

She showed them to the child, and said the child picked out the defendant and the co-defendant. But she didn't think it important to show them to anyone else. Who is she trying to protect? Who is she trying to hide? She didn't give the names, because they didn't ask her for the names. That's what she said.

As I indicated to you during the opening, we didn't have many witnesses. The Commonwealth always has more witnesses than the defense. But there are two important witnesses that have been in this court the whole time, number one is common sense, and number two is human nature.

Now the Commonwealth would have you to believe that this child was vaginally intercoursed, anally intercoursed and orally intercoursed repeatedly. As I indicated ladies and gentlemen, two important witnesses have been here the whole time, common sense and human nature.

But they want you to believe, from the child, that it happened five times, from the detective that it happened nine or ten times. And there was no evidence. No there might not have been any evidence two years later, but there certainly would have been evidence around the time that type of act happened repeatedly to this child.

And then the child said it didn't hurt. Use your own common sense. Use your own common sense. By now you must have great doubts about this case, and I ask that when you go back to the jury room that you raise those doubts.

We promised you and asked you not to let sympathy, either

for the child or for the defendant, decide the case. This man is proud and respectable, and has been a member of the United States military. He is not looking for sympathy. What he wants today is justice, not sympathy.

And no, Pettina Asher is not on trial here today. But her credibility, her character, and the most important thing, what the child told her is in question. And I submit to you that the Commonwealth has failed to prove to you by competent meaningful testimony that she is a believable witness.

The guilt of the defendant cannot be presumed. It can be guessed on. It cannot be speculated on. And do you wonder, and does it raise doubt in your mind, as to why very little investigation took place in this case?

Maybe the CHR Department and the Louisville Police Department didn't think it was a very important case. The Detective told you he only interviewed the mother and the child one time. No follow-up evidence whatsoever.

Didn't try to go get the blanket that was allegedly used. Didn't ask or receive the photographs that were allegedly shown. Didn't interview anybody else that might have been living there, and who had access to this child. Didn't interview the grandmother, except by telephone, and that was not a part of his notes, and they were not brought in here today. CHR didn't interview the grandmother, a most important witness, because she was the first one that the child allegedly told what somebody did to her.

Reasonable doubt has been mentioned several times and the judge has instructed you, and it says [*Hagan reading*] If you have any reasonable doubt on any element of these offenses or, on the whole case, then you shall find him not guilty. And I would submit that just one, one single solitary reasonable doubt is sufficient for you to find him not guilty.

And they want us to believe that the child remembers and was totally composed as to what she told him. But she got on the stand and right at the beginning the judge asked her, and she said, "Do you promise to tell the truth today"? And then Kelly Miller asked her, "Did anyone else bother you, and she said no. And five minutes later, she indicated that someone else bothered her.

Now right there you have to have a doubt as to her honesty and her believability. And you heard her say that her mother told her where this happened. And I would submit that if the mother told her where it happened, her mother could have also told her who did it, and when it happened. She could remember when and who, but she couldn't remember where.

The mother stated emphatically that the defendant gave this child a bath. And you heard the child, in her own words, and I believe she raised her voice a little, "The defendant never gave me a bath!" The mother says this happened at night. The child says emphatically, no!

Just think from what the mother told you how many times this child was and could have been left alone. How many different people were there and could have had access to this child. The numerous relations, the numerous boyfriends, the numerous flings, and that should raise some doubt in your mind.

You know children are more imaginative than adults, and children are more susceptible to suggestion than adults. Children's approximation of dates, times, events, and people is often more unreliable than adults. And you heard her say, that she never saw the pictures before and never saw them afterwards.

Ladies and gentlemen of the jury, all twelve of you, you cannot convict the defendant on conjecture. You cannot convict him on the belief that he might have done it. You can't convict him on speculation. It is not enough to say he's probably or possibly guilty. That would violate all concepts of decency and fairness.

Reasonable doubt doesn't contemplate possibilities or probabilities, as the Commonwealth would have you to believe. What kind of country would we live in if people went to the penitentiary because we thought they were guilty? The sound principles upon which our constitution and our system of justice are based would not tolerate guilt by belief or suspicion.

A man must be proven guilty beyond a reasonable doubt. And the law and the oath to which you swore says to the Commonwealth, represented by Kelly Miller, that you must establish this defendant's guilt by credible and believable testimony from witnesses, and you must do so beyond a reasonable doubt.

The evidence must be clear that it establishes beyond a doubt found in reason that this person committed this act. From the evidence alone, not from what we think might have happened, not from what must have happened, not from there is no other way it could have happened, and if the child says it happened it happened.

All of you are honest and civic minded and you can appreciate that in a criminal case, unlike a civil case as we explained to you, there is no monetary penalty here. You find him guilty, and a person committing these acts deserves to go to the penitentiary. And that's why the law places a heavy burden on the Commonwealth.

Because once you have retired to that jury room and rendered a verdict, and you are not sure, and you have some reservations, and you believe the prosecution has left out some missing link, and you believe that somebody else could have touched this child, and this child is obviously mistaken, then you have to give the benefit of all of those doubts to my client and return a verdict of not guilty.

I ask you go in the jury room, and if you have doubts, point them out to your fellow jurors, whether it comes from something I said, something you heard, or something you've elicited from the testimony. Tell them about any doubts that you have.

Finally I believe you must say to the Commonwealth that there is insufficient evidence in this case to find this man guilty of sodomy, and he deserves to go free. Ladies and gentlemen, I ask you, I implore you, I beseech you to do what is right and just and fair in this, case and return a verdict of not guilty.

A few years from now hopefully you can look back and say: "I know that my decision was right, I know that my decision was just, and justice will have prevailed. But if anyone of you later says, "I think, I hope I made the right decision, a grave wrong, a grave injustice may have been done.

And to each of you, I do not believe that the evidence in this case says to you that the Commonwealth has proved this case beyond a reasonable doubt. I ask that you stand and stand forever if necessary back in that jury room. Stand on what you believe and what you know is right. Stand by what is right and do not compromise with what is wrong. Thank you very much!

CASE #3

Date of verdict:	March 2, 1994
Charge:	Wanton Endangerment 1st Class D Felony
Possible sentence:	1 to 5 years
Judge:	Hon. Geoffrey Morris, Jefferson Circuit Court
Prosecutors:	Hon. Ms. Heidelman & Hon. Mr. Hickey
Defendant's opening statement:	10 minutes
Commonwealth's closing argument:	25 minutes
Defendant's closing argument:	19 minutes
Reasonable Doubt used	9 times
Length of jury deliberations:	2 hours, 10 minutes
Was defendant a convicted felon?	NO
Did defendant testify?	YES
Verdict:	**NOT GUILTY**

SYNOPSIS

The defendant was indicted on charges of Wanton Endangerment and Terroristic Threatening resulting from an incident on July 1, 1993 in Louisville, Jefferson County, KY. The defendant entered a plea and was to be probated. The judge rejected the plea agreement, and indicated he would order the defendant to jail. The defendant was allowed to withdraw his plea and go to trial.

That evening the defendant was sitting in his car in the parking lot of the Service Merchandise Store on Shelbyville Road waiting on his wife and daughter to return from King's Island Amusement Park in Cincinnati, OH. Also present in the parking lot were three undercover narcotics officers, waiting for drug money to be delivered for an undercover drug operation that was to take place nearby.

Approximately thirty minutes after the defendant arrived in the parking lot, Detective Mahaffey walked towards his car on his way to the McDonald's next door. The Detective said that the defendant verbally threatened him, then removed a tire iron from his trunk and threatened him physically. The defendant said that he was apprehensive about the man walking across the dark parking lot toward his car, and asked what the detective wanted. The defendant then reached into his trunk for the tire iron.

The defendant denied that he swung the tire jack at the detective. The defendant said he was slammed to the ground as his daughter and wife turned the corner while on the church bus. When the officers identified themselves, the defendant immediately surrendered and was arrested.

After a two day trial, the judge directed a verdict on the charge of terroristic threatening. The defendant did testify in the case. After 3 to 4 hours of deliberation, the jury found the defendant **NOT GUILTY** of Wanton Endangerment I, Wanton Endangerment II and Menacing.

OPENING STATEMENT

Ladies and gentlemen, when people differ in their versions of what happened regarding an incident, many questions often go unanswered. But you as a jury, today and tomorrow, will decide what happened on July 27, out there at the Service Merchandise on Shelbyville Road.

Now as the judge has told you, opening argument or opening statement is like a road map. And it is just that. It is a roadmap to help you follow the evidence as it comes in and put it in its place. What I say is not evidence, just as what Ms. Heidelman says is not evidence. But the purpose here is to kind of give you a map or a guide.

Have you ever gone on a trip and before you go, you either go up to triple AAA and get routed, or you pull out an old map and look at your route. That's what we try to do in opening statement, just give you a little road map as to where we will be going with the evidence, and what the evidence will show.

You are the triers of fact in this case. The evidence will come from the witness stand and the Judge will give you the law at the end of the case.

Now what do we believe the evidence will show as it relates to this defendant. On July 31st, an ordinary summer afternoon, he went out to the Service Merchandise on Shelbyville Road, right near the McDonalds, for the express purpose of meeting his wife who was coming back from King's Island with some kids. He left his home out in southern Jefferson County. He had his two little twin girls with him in the car. They had prearranged that he would meet that van there sometime about 10:00 or 9:30 or 10:30, as they were coming back from King's Island

He did not leave home expecting or anticipating any trouble. He didn't leave home with any weapons. He did not have any drugs. He was not part of this deal that was going down with these officers and some other unknown individual. He was there for one purpose, to meet this van. And his every intention was to meet this van, and get whoever he was to take in his car and go back home.

He pulled into the lot. He pulls over near the McDonald's and the evidence will show that he backs into the parking space. He didn't pull in frontward, or he didn't go through the McDonald's drive-thru, because he wasn't there to get food. He was merely there to wait for the van that was to come off the interstate highway.

Now he did notice three guys sitting over there in a car. Sitting or standing, there may be some dispute as to what they were doing, but they were over there near a car, and that car was a couple of rows, or a row or two away two away from his car. He sat there for awhile, as Ms. Heideleman told you. They had been there about forty-five minutes. He sat there about thirty minutes.

Then all of a sudden, one of the officers or this detective gets out of the car, and proceeds to go towards the McDonalds, which is directly in the path of his car. Now he is moving at that point at a pretty rapid pace. And this young man gets out of his car and asks the person what he wants.

Now I'll remind you that all of this happened around 9:30 p.m. or 10:00 p.m. It was pretty dark out there. The parking lot had been pretty well lighted, but it was dark out there because it was nighttime. This officer and the other two officers, nobody was in uniform. There were no uniforms. There were no badges. There was nothing identifying them as police officers. They were not in a police car. There were no lights on the car. There were no markings on the car. They were in an unmarked vehicle. And they were waiting for something to do at some other location that he had nothing to do with.

As he goes towards the car, my client gets out of his vehicle, and asks the detective, "Do you want something or do you need something," because he is coming close to his car where the kids are in the car." The detective says no and he keeps walking. At the time he keeps walking, he begins to put his hand in his pocket, to get out some change, he says, to go in McDonalds and buy a soft drink.

My client doesn't know who this person is, what he is going to do, or what is going on. Its nighttime, it's dark and he's got his two children there. So he goes to the back of his car and opens his trunk, and yes, he did get out a tire jack.

Now I'm not going to touch it. All these other people have touched it, and it's supposed to be evidence. And I don't know whether it's going to be introduced, as to where he grabbed it at, but I don't want to put my fingerprints on it, since everyone else has already touched it.

He took the jack out, and he asked the man, "Do you want something or are you going to mess with me or something"? And the other three officers ran over and pulled out their guns, pulled out their badges, and said "we are police." Now up to that point, nobody had made any identification as to being a police officer. This detective didn't even say "I was going to the McDonald's to buy me a soft drink."

It only took a matter of seconds when all this went down. Now coincidentally, at the same time, this van that he was supposed to meet was pulling in with his wife and these kids off of I-264, going east right at the Shelbyville Road exit. It pulls into the parking lot.

Ms. Black looks over and sees the car sitting there that she is supposed to meet. By the time they go straight up to the Service Merchendise, and turn to the right or come back down the road to come to his car, that's when she notices three guys approaching her husband with guns drawn. And she hollers for somebody to call the police.

She will tell you that she went over and identified herself and said "I'm his wife and supposed to meet the car." Somebody pulled a gun on her and asked her a question, "Is he on drugs, is he high on something, or what is he doing"? They told her to get back, threw him on the ground, and then he got locked up, and that's why we are here today.

The evidence will also show that no one ever got hit by this jack, not this detective, not the other two detectives, no one. EMS was not called. There was no property damage. No one got any clothes torn, no one got any eyeglasses busted.

That's where the stories start to go apart. My client says he didn't swing the jack at all. He merely went back there and got the jack out to protect himself and his kids because he didn't know who this person was. He was in tennis shoes. He was in blue jeans. He was not in a uniform. He didn't have on a coat and tie. He didn't know what this person was going to do. His only purpose in going and getting that jack was to protect himself and his kids, if somebody attempted to do something to them.

There were a lot of people in the van most of them were kids and its no sense dragging them in here. We don't know what they saw. Most of them were sleep. They had been at King's Island all day. Ms. Black will take the stand and tell you what she saw from the moment when that van pulled off of that ramp heading over into the Service Merchandise parking lot.

I will ask you to listen to the evidence. The evidence will also show one other thing. As soon, immediately, in just a matter of seconds when they identified themselves as police officers, he backed up and dropped the jack, immediately. He made no threatening or advancing moves. He didn't' say "I am going to kill you or anything like that." He wasn't throwing trash out of the car. He wasn't playing his music loud because the kids were in the back car sleep. Now they are saying when he came into the lot they saw the kids. I don't know how they could see the kids they were asleep. We are talking about two three year olds.

Now I will ask you to listen to all of the evidence and weigh all of it as it comes from this stand and decide what happened out there on July 31st. I believe you will agree that the defendant is innocent of this charge. Thank You!

CLOSING ARGUMENT

Judge Morris, Mr. Hickey, ladies and gentlemen of the jury, first of all I would like to thank you on behalf of my client, myself and the Court because jury duty and jury service is one of the ways we keep the criminal system going. I know everyone is not always satisfied with what juries do, but without the jury process, I don't know where we would be as a country or as a community. And we'd like to thank you for your service.

It's important that you listen to what I say, because under our rules of court and under our order of procedures, I have to go first, and the prosecutor gets to go last. I don't get to stand up again. We don't get to go back and forth. I get one shot at it and she l get the last shot at it. So it's important you listen to what I say, because my client at this time is speaking to you, through his lawyer.

Remember I told you at the beginning of this case that when people differ in their versions of what happened on an incident, a lot of questions often go unanswered. That's important because when you really size up the evidence that's been presented in this case, it comes down to two people. It comes down to Detective Mahaffey, who is a fine detective, and it comes down to this defendant

Now the prosecutor may stand up here and say or paint you a picture, "well it's just a matter of whether you believe him, or whether you believe him. "And if you believe him he's guilty, if you believe him he's not guilty." And I would submit to you it is not that simple.

And that's because we've had other people in here testifying. We've had this other Detective Jeffries. We've had Lt. Fitzgerald, who is still here. And we have had both the defendant's wife and the defendant testify. But all of what they have told you happened in the Service Merchandise lot is really not in conflict. We may be a car or two away from where these people were parked.

There might be some conflict as to the way he went into the McDonald's. But what is important, is what happened right here at the car. Whether the car was here, or whether the car was here. That's what important in this case.

And that is important because what happened happened at a most crucial time. It happened at a time that the other officer's attention was diverted for some reason. They were doing something else. When the detective decided to go get a soft drink, they were looking somewhere else. They were facing somewhere else. They were not looking at him at the crucial moment when this happened. He had to yell. That's when they struck into action immediately and went over there. So they didn't see what happened up to that point.

It's also important because we all know it was dark out there.

Now there are lights in the parking lot, and these photographs have been introduced by the Commonwealth as exhibits #3 and #4. But these photographs were taken during the day. It was night out there. It was dark. It was ten o lock at night. Even in July it's still dark at ten o lock at night.

This man is there and there for one reason only, even by their own admission, by their witnesses. He is there sitting in his car. Their witness came in and said, "Nothing out of the ordinary was going on. Nothing happened until this officer got up to go over to the McDonald's."

Now I believe the prosecutor asked a question, or a question was asked, "Did he have to go by this car to get there"? Well he didn't have to go by this car to get there. He could have gone down this way and that way. There are a number of ways he could have got there.

We know now that Ms. Green didn't here what was said. We know that the other two detectives did not hear any of the words that were exchanged between Detective Mahaffey and the defendant.

Now what does Mark know? He knows that he is waiting on his wife and kids from approximately the same spot that he dropped them off. He knows that it's dark. He knows that he's been sitting there thirty minutes. And he sees the biggest of these three officers coming towards him.

And as he is coming towards him one of his hands are in his pocket, and he's fiddling with something. He doesn't know what is about to happen, or who this person is, or what this person is going to do. He is moving towards the defendant, and while he is moving towards him, his two twin girls are in the back of the car. Now I think at that point it is reasonable for him to think that something might occur. Something might happen at that point.

And what did he do? He went around to the back of the car, as he told you, and opened his trunk and got a jack out. Now that's the first time I have touched this jack. Everybody else has touched it before, and it was introduced as evidence. I don't know why fingerprints were not taken. Fingerprints surely could have been lifted off of that jack, which would have let you know, without a doubt, whether or not he was holding this jack with one or two hands. Why didn't they take fingerprints? Why didn't they preserve it like all other evidence is preserved? It's even taped up, and that is not the condition it was found in when they took it off of the ground.

He's in fear. He has some alarm, natural instinct. He goes and gets something to ward off any danger to himself or to his kids. The officer yells, and reaches around, even though he admitted to you he didn't have a weapon in his pocket, he reaches around and the other officers spring into action. They say police drop it. Drop the "f" weapon or whatever. He steps back and drops it. Now whether he dropped it one second later, or two seconds later, he immediately dropped it. And that's what you'd expect him to do. I know if three people were holding a gun on me, I would drop anything that I was holding.

Now these Instructions that the Court has given you, Wanton Endangerment I [*Hagan pointing to Instruction #1*] The only way that you can find this defendant guilty under this Instruction, first you have to find under "A" that he swung a car jack. And I believe that's in dispute here, as to whether he swung a car jack. He says he didn't swing it, he says he swung it. And, after you find that he swung it, you have to find that he thereby created a substantial danger of death or serious physical injury. I would submit to you there was no substantial danger of death because all of them were armed.

And you heard what the one detective told you, he thought he was going to have to shoot him. Now they want you to believe that he kept advancing on the detectives with this weapon, while they've got 9mm's trained on him. And one of them even has it cocked.

I don't believe there was a substantial of danger of death or serious physical injury to those detectives. They were well equipped. They were going on a drug buy. They were going on a drug operation. You know they are armed. You know they are well prepared to protect themselves. And then if you find those two, you have to also find under "B" that under the circumstances, such conduct manifested an extreme indifference to the value of human life

Now what is an extreme indifference to the value of human life, protecting yourself or preparing to protect yourself or your kids? I don't think that is an extreme indifference to the value of human life. Maybe somebody walking into the courtroom and pointing a loaded weapon, or shooting into an occupied vehicle, or shooting into the front door of somebody's house. That kind of conduct is extreme. I don't think there was any conduct in this case that was extreme on the defendant's part.

He told you of a situation that he had been in where he had been mugged before. The prosecutor wanted to make light of the fact that he may have not reported it. And even when the jury was questioned, she asked some of you whether you had reported some of those things. And some of you said yes, and some people said no. A lot of crimes, a lot of muggings, and a lot of assaults often go unreported.

But then we get to the critical point of what happened at the car, that's when the stories start to diverge. [*Hagan pointing his hands outward in v shape*] And then the Court has instructed you here under Instruction #7 [*Hagan reading reasonable doubt instruction*] you shall find the defendant not guilty unless you are satisfied from the evidence alone...

Not from what you think might have happened, not from what probably could have happened, not from what may have happened, but from the evidence alone and beyond a reasonable doubt that he is guilty. And if upon the whole case, when you look at this whole situation, these whole circumstances, if upon the whole case you have a reasonable doubt that he is guilty, then you shall find him not guilty.

The Commonwealth, as we told you at the beginning of this case, has the burden of proof. We don't have to prove that he didn't do it. We don't have to prove anything. We didn't have to have him take the stand. He elected to take the stand and tell you what happened out there on July 31. They have to prove it, and they have to prove it beyond a reasonable doubt as to each of these offenses.

And the court has also instructed you on the charge of Wanton Endangerment in the Second Degree. And again [*Hagan reading Wanton Endangerment II Instruction*] you have got to find, not two things but three things. You've got to find that he swung a car jack, and you've got to find that he thereby wantonly created a substantial danger of physical injury to Dan Mahaffey.

Now this car jack is kind of heavy, and I would submit to you that somebody swinging this car jack has to hold it with two hands. Now we don't have the evidence here to show how many of his hands were on this car jack. If he was swinging this car jack with that much force, or as many times as they say, isn't it reasonable to believe that that would slip down, or that he would lose his balance. Isn't that reasonable?

You might get back there in the jury room and say, "Well, I know what this side says, and I know what this side says. But do I really know what happened in this case"? And I would submit to you that when you look at this Instruction on reasonable doubt, that it will spring into your mind, that there is some reasonable doubt in my mind.

Have they proved it beyond a reasonable doubt? Now this case didn't take very long as most cases do. Most cases up here take two and three days. It didn't involve many witnesses. You usually have thirty or forty witnesses, and you have ten and twenty exhibits. This case didn't take very long. It didn't involve many witnesses. But I don't want you to take it from the length of the case or from the brevity of it that it's not an important case. It is a very important case.

What you decide by your verdict back there in that jury room will follow this young man for the rest of his life, him and his family. Five or six years from now, I guess I will still be practicing law, here or somewhere else, the judge will be in retirement, Ms. Heidelmn will still be a prosecutor.

Five or six years from now I want you to look back on this day and say, " I know I did what was right in that case. I went back there. I didn't rush to judgment. I listened to my other jurors. I expressed my own opinions. I stood on my own convictions." I ask you to go back there and do what is right in this case.

Stand if you have to stand alone. Whatever the amount of time it takes you back there, use that time to come back with the right verdict and don't rush to an incomplete and quick verdict, just to get it over with, because it is very important to this gentleman.

Now the judge has also instructed you on the third charge menacing. And in order to find him guilty of menacing, you have to find two things. [*Hagan reading instruction on menacing*] "That in Jefferson County on that day, he intentionally placed Dan Mahaffey in reasonable fear of immediate physical injury by swinging a car jack. And that in so doing he was not privileged to act in self-protection." So if you find the first one you, still can't convict him until you find the second one. And the self-protection one is very important, and I want to read that one to you.

[*Hagan reading instruction on self-protection*] Because even though the defendant might otherwise be found guilty under instruction #3, if at the time the defendant swung the jack, if he did so, if he did so, he believed that Dan Mahaffey was about to use physical force upon him, he was privileged. That means the law gives him a privilege, the law gives him the right to use such physical force against Dan Mahaffey, as he believed to be necessary to protect himself against it. If he has the right to protect himself, he certainly has the right to protect his children. That's what self defense and self protection are all about. He was justified in what he was doing for his own protection.

And he didn't exceed the force that was necessary, because when they asked him to drop it, he dropped it immediately. Now if he continued on and continued swinging it you're right. We probably wouldn't be here today, because some other result would have happened.

I would submit to you that he acted out of nothing more than what is the universal law of nature. Every species is endowed with the instinct of self preservation and self protection. That a man has an absolute right to defend himself from personal danger and personal harm cannot be disputed.

His action was defensive and I believe it was appropriate for the circumstances he found at the time. His action was reasonable under the circumstances. I don't think he exceeded what he needed to do to let them know that you are not going to do anything to me, or you are not going to do anything to my children.

There is no evidence been brought in here that he is a violent, high tempered or angry man. You've heard that he is a man that works three jobs, that has two children of his own that live with him, and a step-child, three jobs to take care, to take care of his family. Anybody that was going out there to cause trouble, would they take their two or three year old twin daughters with them? If he was anticipating trouble, didn't he know if these officers are coming at him with guns and if he continued advancing on the officers, as they want you to believe, a stray bullet could have hit one of the children? He dropped the weapon immediately when they asked him to drop it.

Finally I would ask you to keep several promises (1) that you wouldn't use the indictment as evidence, you wouldn't allow sympathy or prejudice, sympathy or prejudice for this officer, sympathy or prejudice for this defendant to affect your verdict, and (2) that you would decide this case on the facts from that witness chair and the evidence alone.

And you also promised us and you said you understood that the commonwealth has the burden in this case. We don't have to do anything. They have to prove him guilty, and they have to prove him guilty beyond a reasonable doubt. That is what the law requires you to do, and that is what these Instructions require you to do.

If you have a reasonable doubt, then point it out to your other fellow jurors. Let them know what your doubts are about this case. Now you might say, "well there is some evidence about throwing trash outside of the car or loud music, or what kind of music he was playing, or all at that."

I don't think that evidence was very important. It has nothing to do with the critical events around the car. You heard the officer say he only told the prosecutor about it day before trial. If it was important, why didn't they charge him with it? They had two extra lines on the arrest slip. They certainly could have written in two extra things, if it was important. Now whose credibility is at issue there?

No, that's just to cloud the issues. He's throwing trash out, so he's a bad person. He's polluting the environment, he's playing loud music, and he is disturbing other people. You heard me ask all of the questions? Were there any complaints from anybody or any stores that he was bothering anybody? You heard the detective testify, "nothing out of the ordinary happened."

Keep focus on what is at issue here, him swinging the jack and why he swung it. He told you why he swung it. He was there and there for one reason only to meet his wife and children. He was there to pick them up. He had his two children with him. He perceived a danger or fear to himself, and he acted out of self instinct.

Extreme indifference means he would have kept on at all odds. Extreme indifference means he would have run after somebody. You've heard no testimony that he ran after anybody with that. You've heard no testimony that he threw that at anybody. I ask you to look at all the evidence, to weigh the evidence carefully, and I ask you to return a verdict of not guilty on all charges in this case. Thank you.

CASE #4

Date of verdict:	September 30, 1994
Charges:	Criminal Mischief 1st Class D Felony; Violation of Graves, First Offense, Class A Misdemeanor
Possible sentences:	1 to 5 years; 12 months in jail and/or $500 fine
Judge:	Hon. William Knopf, Jefferson Circuit Court
Prosecutor:	Hon. Micah Guilfoil & Hon. Mr. Hickey
Defendants opening statement:	10 minutes
Defendant's closing argument:	20 minutes
Commonwealth's closing argument:	7 minutes
Reasonable Doubt used	15 times
Length of jury deliberations:	2 hours, 50 minutes
Was defendant a convicted felon?	NO
Did defendant testify?	NO
Verdict:	NOT GUILTY*

* Trial included six defendants, all of whom were acquitted of all charges

SYNOPSIS

The defendant, along with four other defendants, were each charged with 24 counts of Grave Desecration and Criminal Mischief. These charges stemmed from the alleged wanton or intentional damaging of 465 tombstones, monuments, and headstones in Eastern Cemetery during March 6, and May 15, 1993. The Cemetery sits at the east end of Broadway next to beautiful Cave Hill Cemetery in Louisville, KY.

This cemetery was in operation before 1900 and it is estimated to contain some 40,000+ graves. Newspaper and television reports, long before the alleged vandalization, reported that persons were buried two and three deep. In 1991, a human skull was stolen from a grave. There were numerous problems with homeless people sleeping in the cemetery. The cemetery had been virtually abandoned by the management. In the early 1990's a Judge ordered the cemetery to not take in any more bodies. The trust fund allegedly set up by the owners of the cemetery had no money in it for perpetual grave care as required by state law.

While some of the defendants admitting knocking over some tombstones, this defendant denied everything. Even some of the tombstones were too heavy to be knocked over by humans. They had obviously been knocked over by equipment that was disinterring and reinterring bodies to other cemeteries, and to the cemetery next door. By the time of trial, the cemetery was in receivership with the Court. A Circuit Court Judge (Ken Conliffe) was called to testify about the cemetery about the deplorable conditions and mismanagement.

The defendant did not testify. After a four-day trial, the judge instructed the jury on Criminal mischief 1st, 2nd, and 3rd. The jury returned a verdict of **NOT GUILTY** on each of the four counts and for all six defendants.

OPENING STATEMENT

Judge Knopf, Ms Guilfoil, fellow counsel, ladies and gentlemen of the jury. The Commonwealth has just made an admission to you that some of its witnesses are confused. The evidence in this case is going to that a lot of their witnesses are confused. You are in this court room as part of your constitutional obligation. And your obligation is to do justice, to do the right thing as to each of these defendants, particularly the defendant I represent. That is the oath to which you have just sworn.

The purpose of these opening statements, as the judge says, this is not evidence. This is just our chance to give you a little road map. Have you ever taken a trip and before you go you get out a map or go to Triple AAA and have them to route you? This is kind of a routing as to show you where the evidence will go. What I say is not evidence, just as what the prosecutor says cannot be evidence. The evidence will come from the witness stand.

You are the triers of fact. You will determine what happened in that cemetery between the dates of March 6, 1993 and May 15, 1993. You will determine whether the Commonwealth can prove him guilty beyond a reasonable doubt as to Criminal Mischief 1st degree, and as to desecration of graves

What the prosecution did not tell you but what I will tell you is nobody put a whole in the fence. These young men didn't go through a hole in the fence. Why didn't they just go through the front gate which is always open? This cemetery is in court receivership. It has no management. It has no security. The gates are not locked. There is no one in the office. The office is completely closed and locked. There are no utilities on in the office. No one is running the cemetery, except under the receivership of the court.

There is a back gate to the cemetery that is always open. Now why would they have to crawl through an opening or a hole, when the cemetery is open day and night, and has been for years? What they also will not tell you is that there are several bars around the cemetery. Phoenix Hill Tavern is directly across the street on Baxter Avenue. Cliff Hangers, another bar. Spring Street tavern, another bar and Baxter Station.

The cemetery being open, you have a lot of people in and out of these bars, a lot of people that are intoxicated. People go in and out of the cemetery all the time, the evidence will show that. The evidence will also show you that homeless people sleep in the cemetery. The evidence will also show you that the cemetery is in receivership and some people who have loved ones buried in the cemetery disinter the body. That means to have the body dug up and removed to another cemetery. How do you dig a body up? Well, you take in a backhoe, and you dig up the dirt and the gravel, and what ever else is there down to six feet and remove it.

Don't you think in doing all of that there would be damage to other monuments and other tombstones, particularly when you have a cemetery with space for 15,000, but that has 80,000 bodies buried in it, and was basically full at the turn of the century?

And then you have volunteers in the cemetery day and night. If you have loved ones there, like I do, you go in the cemetery, and you mow the lawn, you mow the grass, you clean around the grave of your loved ones. Inexperienced people, handling lawn equipment, helping to preserve or stabilize, or helping to beautify the place where their loved ones are buried.

Now what will the evidence will show in this case as to this defendant? Once the police had taken statements from a number of people, talked to a number of people, and you will hear ranges anywhere from twenty people to as many as sixty people being in the cemetery yet we only have six people here today. And you will hear of people that have moved out of town that were in the cemetery. The Commonwealth surely knows how to bring somebody back if they committed a crime. Where are those people at since we only have six here today. There were females in the cemetery. We have no females. We have all males. Did somebody make a decision that there involvement was less so they are not going to be tried?

What did the police do? Oh they took some statements from some people. They told some guys, "if you don't tell us or give some names you are going to the penitentiary." This defendant didn't make a statement. He exercised his right to remain silent and remained silent. He didn't give the police a statement, even though they scared him. You will have to look at each of these statements, implicating some and not implicating other people, and add the weight that you want to those statements.

I'd asked you to look for one basic thing. Is there any date in any one of those statements given to the police? You would expect if the police were going to take a statement they would at least ask, "well what dates are you talking about." If you say someone was in the cemetery, what dates are you talking about? I'll ask you to examine and remember as each one of those statements come in. Listen for the dates because the dates are crucial. We are not talking about anything that happened in 1991, 1992, or even 1994. We are specifically talking about March 6 through May 15, 1993.

The Commonwealth also told you about 465 tombstones. I ask you to keep 465 tombstones in your mind because that's the compass you have to judge their evidence by. That's the star that you need to keep looking at, 465 tombstones. Can they prove that he, either acting alone or with these other people, damaged 465 tombstones? I also ask you to look at the evidence and we believe that the evidence will show there is no evidence that he mutilated any fences. I ask you to remember the evidence about fences, shrubbery, ornaments, or that he removed the flowers placed on anyone's grave.

Now often times when people differ in their versions of what happened on a given date or a given incident, that's why we have juries. You are here to sort out what happened on those particular days. The police jumped to the wrong conclusion in this case. They jumped to the wrong conclusion, and why do I say that in this case. Because the evidence will show, after they talked to all of the people, they didn't do anything else. They did not go back to any of the merchants that are located around Eastern Cemetery, and see whether they had witnessed, heard, or seen anything. They didn't go next door to Cave Hill Cemetery, to see if the guard had heard anything, or to see if the dogs had been awakened by all of the commotion going on in the cemetery. I ask you to judge the weight and the credibility of that testimony as it comes in. They didn't pass out any fliers seeking to find any witnesses to these particular events.

We are talking about six specific dates March 6, March 20, March 27, April 25, April 29, and May 15 of 1993. Those are the only dates we are talking about, no other dates and no other times. I do not believe that there will be one shred of evidence that this defendant either wantonly or intentionally damaged or destroyed any monuments, headstones, tombstones, foot stones, or markers.

And the Commonwealth is going to show you photographs. Again, I ask you to hold their feet to the fire. Make them connect the photograph with the witness that is on the stand, and say what this defendant did as to each tombstone or monument in each one of those photographs. We do not believe there will be any evidence that can connect this defendant with any one of those monuments or tombstones.

I ask you to sit and hear the evidence impartially as it comes from the witness stand, and I believe that you will be convinced that the Commonwealth has not met its burden, and you will return a verdict of not guilty as to this defendant. Thank you very much.

CLOSING ARGUMENT

May it please the Court, Ms. Guilfoil, Mr. Hickey fellow counsel ladies and gentlemen of the jury, I was going first and now we are reversed. *[There were five lawyers for the six defendants and Mr. Hagan was the last to close]* And since I am going last, so you might wonder what kind of things I might say that these fine lawyers have not already said.

Be that as it may, let me add my thanks on behalf of myself, as an officer of the Court, and this kid, the defendant. Will you stand up *[the defendant stands]*? Remember him when you go back to the jury room. His wife is here, and Charlotte, thank you for coming.

You know most stories have one beginning and one end, but a trial has two beginnings and two endings. Our job is about over and yours is about to begin. Remember back during my opening or in jury selection, and I said, you have a solemn task, a simple but a solemn task, to do justice, to do the right thing in this case.

Now under our system the Commonwealth always gets to go last, so it's important for you to listen to what I say. It is very important that you pay attention because neither I nor any of these other five lawyers will have a chance to get back up. So it is very important. I will be the last person speaking on behalf of this defendant, but really on behalf of all these five defendants.

Now at the beginning of this case, we asked you several things; whether you understood that the indictment, even though it was read to you by the prosecution, is not evidence. We asked you whether you understood that the presumption of innocence comes into this courthouse, with these individuals, and follows them into this courtroom, and stays with them throughout the trial. You said you understood that. And the judge has given you that in these Instructions, presumption of innocence, and that the indictment is not any weight.

Now we also asked you whether you understood that it would be necessary for us to object and to vigorously cross examine the witnesses. And that's our job as lawyers. That's the oath to which we swore. And that you wouldn't hold it against our clients, if you didn't like something we did, or if we objected too much, or thought we cross examined a witness too vigorously. You said you understood that, and you said you could follow that.

Two things you can judge this case on: the law as given to you by the Judge in these Instructions, and the facts--the facts that come from the witness chair.

And finally you said you understood that the amount of proof that is necessary to convict a person in a criminal case is a very high standard, and that is proof beyond a reasonable doubt. And that proof, proof beyond a reasonable doubt, has to come from the Commonwealth's side alone, not from this side, *[Hagan pointing to Commonwealth Attorney]* but from this side alone.

That proof has to convince you, and convince each one of you, beyond a reasonable doubt as to each of these defendants, and as to each element of the offenses for which they are charged. The Commonwealth alone has to paint the complete picture for you.

Now my client is married has been married six years and works at Fischer Packing Company. You might have seen him in here with that arm band on. That's because he cut his hand, he's a butcher. He has to take care of two children and a wife. He doesn't have time to run around in the cemetery and play childish games.

Even though plenty of them have admitted they might have been in there sometimes previously, he's got relatives buried there. If anybody's got a right to be angry about what's going on at Eastern cemetery, it is people with relatives buried there.

And I have relatives buried there, so I've got a right to be angry. But I am not so angry that I want to send any one of these six gentlemen to the penitentiary on this type of evidence, evidence that is wholly insufficient, evidence that is not beyond the standard of proof, which is proof beyond a reasonable doubt.

Now during my opening, I promised you several things. I promised you we would show you that the cemetery was open day and night. And that was agreed to, even by the Commonwealth's witnesses, Mr. Keith, Bob Winlock, and it was confirmed by Judge Conliffe, who they brought in.

No security or management, lots of mismanagement, years of vandalism and mismanagement, disinterments and reinterments, and homeless people sleeping there. The cemetery is used as a shortcut to the Save A Step Food Market, or to bars that are close by. And a number of ways to get in and out.

I believe we showed you all of these things that I promised we would show you. I ask you to judge whether we kept our promises. Now the Commonwealth also made you some promises, and as I usually do, I write down what the Commonwealth says in its opening.

The first thing they promised you is that they would show you that these six defendants snuck in through the fence. Have you heard any proof that they snuck in? Why would they have to sneak in when it is open day and night?

The next thing they said was they would show was that these acts were intentional and wanton. Do you ever remember the question being asked of any witness? No, not of any witness. Not their star witness, Charles Salee.

Were these acts done intentionally or were these acts done wantonly? You can only find them guilty, if you believe from the evidence alone, that the acts were intentional or wanton. Where is that evidence that the Commonwealth said they would prove to you?

And finally they admitted, I had to look up because I didn't believe it, that some of their witnesses would be confused Yes, a lot of their witnesses were confused. Somebody said the cemetery was very neat. I think Mr. Winlock says it was in good condition. And then Mr. Keith from the monument company comes in and says, "The condition of that cemetery was horrendous."

It is obvious that the Commonwealth has defaulted on the promise they made to each one of you, as far as this defendant, and the other five defendants are concerned. Instead of honoring the promise they made to you, they have given you a bad check, a check that has come back marked "insufficient evidence, and not evidence beyond a reasonable doubt."

The writer *James Baldwin* once said, "*The moment we break faith with one another or with our promises, the sea engulfs us, and the lights goes out.*" And I believe that the light has gone out on the Commonwealth in this case.

Now these Instructions say, as to the defendant, and one other defendant, that you cannot hold it against him, or use it as evidence against him in any way, the fact that he did not testify. And he did not testify. And that is a decision made by him, in consultation with me as his lawyer. But you can't use that as evidence against him, or in any way use that to prejudice your decision in this case, the fact that he did not testify.

But these Instructions clearly say that you must be satisfied from the evidence, and the evidence alone, and beyond a reasonable doubt. Not from inferences, not from hunches, not from guesswork. Not from a hunch, "Well if they were there and the other ones were there, they probably kicked some over too." Not from, "Well if the cemetery is damaged, there is no other way if could have happened, they must have done it." But from the evidence alone and beyond a reasonable doubt, that's the compass or the star that has to guide your deliberations.

And then it finally says, [*Hagan reading instruction*] if upon the whole case, if you look at this whole case, just step back and look at it, if upon the whole case, you have a reasonable doubt that he is guilty, you shall find him not guilty.

Now shall is a mandatory word. You have no option there. If upon the whole case you have a reasonable doubt that he is guilty, you shall find him not guilty. Now I cannot define reasonable doubt either. But we can look at the evidence to see if there are some areas where you can find doubt in this case.

Now the Commonwealth has to climb a very high hill called reasonable doubt. They are the ones that have to move up that mountain. You know there is an old saying out West "If you get to a hill or mountain and want to climb it, waiting, doesn't make the hill or mountain any smaller." Weren't you just waiting for somebody to come into the door and connect one of these six defendants with 465 tombstones?

Maybe that's why the Commonwealth got up and objected when we brought in at [*Hagan pointing to chart*] least some representation of Eastern cemetery, to show you what it was, or give you some idea of what it looked like. They didn't bring in a map or chart. They can't tell you where it happened, what happened, or even when it happened in that cemetery. Now I believe it was *Will Rogers* that said *"Even if you are on the right track, you'll get run over if you just sit there."* The police certainly sat on this one.

This was not a shoddy or sloppy investigation. There was no investigation. One set of photos. We got six incidents and one set of photographs. No interviews of the area residents or the area businesses or the people that maintain the beautiful cemetery next door. No dates on any of the rights waiver forms. No dates on many of the statements. No locations. No times.

Of course, if we knew when and where, we might know who and what? Who did the damage, and the damage to what tombstone? And whether that damage totals a thousand dollars, or five hundred dollars?

Have you heard any witness come in here and put a dollar amount on any tombstone that he damaged? Or say he damaged seven tombstones at X amount of dollars, that totals up to a thousand dollars as to any of these defendants?

Everybody that came in and testified, with the exception of Detective Carroll, nobody brought any reports or any notes. Nobody brought any files. Nobody brought any notes. Everybody is just testifying off the cuff.

And they want you to believe that some of the statements made by these young men, when they are taken down and interrogated, in what the police officer calls "a ceremony", they want you to believe that these statements implicate all these defendants, when some of the statements clearly say, and you will take them to the jury room-- innocent . One young man was questioned twice, and he wrote the same thing--innocent. "Was not there in 1993, was not there in 1992." Yes, "even if you are on the right track, if you just sit there you will get run over."

Let's let the Commonwealth explain why they didn't bring in any of the four juveniles that pled guilty, that paid restitution, and were supposed to do some volunteer work.

Let's let them explain why? Remember because we don't have any burden. We don't have to do anything. They've got to prove it. Why they didn't bring in the kid from California? They went to New Albany to get one of these gentlemen. They didn't go to California to get that kid. Where are the twenty females that were allegedly running in the cemetery, and that their star witness, Charles Salee, says "I guarantee you that females were into it also, knocking over tombstones." Where are the females?

But remember when I got back up and said," I want to make it perfectly clear." I wrote it down. I want you to say who was there, and who knocked over tombstones He didn't knock over any tombstones. That's exactly what he said.

They didn't bring in any of the people living in an apartment in the middle of the cemetery. Can you get a load of that, an apartment in the middle of the cemetery? Isn't it logical to infer that those people might have some parties also? I surely wouldn't want to have a party in that cemetery?

They didn't bring in the Court Receiver. Oh, yes they talked to her, but she has washed her hands of this mess. Remember somebody in the Bible that washed their hands of some mess, that didn't want to get involved. They had any number of ways to get Beth Caldwell down here. Ever heard of a subpoena? That's all they had to do.

And remember the same questions were asked of these six witnesses. You don't know anything about this case, or you don't know anything about any damage to the tombstones? The answers were all the same.

Ladies and gentlemen suspicion is not proof, suspicion is not proof. If you have doubts about this case like I do, when you go back to the jury room, I want you point out those doubts to your fellow jurors. Show your doubts about this case to your fellow jurors.

I would submit to you that one single solitary reasonable doubt is sufficient for you to return a verdict of not guilty on all counts, as to all of these defendants. Let me give you a couple.

DOUBT #1

Dates, times, locations. From the evidence alone now, not from anything else From the evidence alone that places these defendants in that cemetery on those six dates, three dates in March, two dates in April, and one date in May of 1993.

DOUBT #2

Any proof from the evidence alone now. Not from what you think, or not from no other way it could have happened, that any of these six defendants caused a thousand dollars or five hundred dollars damage, traceable directly to each of these defendants.

DOUBT #3

Any proof from the evidence alone that 465 tombstones were damaged by these defendants.

DOUBT #4

Any proof from the evidence alone that these defendants acted, intentionally or wantonly. You heard Sallee's testimony, and if he says, "they were there" and if you conclude they were all there, all there running around in a frenzy, isn't it reasonable to conclude and infer? *[Hagan points to a theme used over and over by the prosecution]*

You don't conclude and infer in a criminal case. You look at the evidence alone that comes from that chair. You know the Commonwealth certainly has a right to build a case on circumstantial evidence. You know the difference between circumstantial and direct. Direct evidence is somebody said, "I saw him do it on such and such a date." Circumstantial evidence is when you put all of these other little pieces together, you don't have anybody directly saying it, but all the circumstances have to be right. I have been practicing law fifteen years, and I wouldn't be practicing now if I didn't know you could build a case on circumstantial evidence. But circumstantial evidence is like a bicycle, it won't go up hill without a chain or peddle.

Finally, when you say to the Commonwealth, at the conclusion of this case, Ms. Guilfoil, Mr. Hickey and the officer, "you have not met your burden," you are still following the law. Just as if the case was clear and simple and the proof was here, you'd be following the law if you convicted them. So don't think that by returning a verdict of not guilty, you are not following the law. You are still following the law.

Finally I ask you, I know its Friday, everybody has got something to do later, today and tomorrow, and the weekend is approaching. But I don't want you to be hasty back there and make a hasty decision, because your decision today will affect all of these young men the rest of their lives. Don't put yourself in a position of having to wrestle later with "Did I do the right thing? Is my conscience clear"?

Sometimes when you stand on principle you have to stand alone. And if that be the case, stand. Stand if you have to stand alone. Stand until hell freezes over. Go back there and do what is right, and do not compromise with what is wrong. Thank You!

CASE #5

Date of verdict:	March 21, 1996
Charges:	Trafficking in Stolen Vehicles and Parts
	Class D Felony
	Theft by Deception over $300
	Class D Felony
	Unauthorized Use of Motor Vehicle,
	Class A Misdemeanor
Possible sentences:	1 to 5 years
	1 to 5 years
	12 months in jail and/or $500 fine
Judge:	Honorable Edwin Schoering
	Jefferson Circuit Court
Prosecutor:	Hon. Craig Dilger

Defendant's opening argument:	6 minutes
Defendant's closing argument:	21 minutes
Commonwealth's closing argument:	18 minutes
Reasonable Doubt used	14 times
Length of jury deliberations:	1 hour, 55 minutes
Was defendant a convicted felon?	YES
Did defendant testify?	NO
Verdict:	**NOT GUILTY**

SYNOPSIS

The defendant was an inmate serving time at Jefferson County Corrections. During the day he was released to go and work at Avis Rent A Car at the Louisville International Airport. He returned to the correctional facility when he got off work.

Automobiles from the Avis Rent a Car started coming up missing and the police apprehended several individuals in several cars. One individual was apprehended and had a 9mm handgun in the vehicle

The people caught in the vehicles said they got them from the defendant for $50.00 with no license, employment information, credit card or other information required. No one ever saw the defendant take or drive any vehicle from the lot, and no one testified that t he defendant was ever missing from work. The defendant was never caught in any of the vehicles

Charges against most of the defendants caught in the cars were dismissed.

The defendant, a convicted felon, did not testify and the jury after deliberating just under two hours, returned a verdict of **NOT GUILTY** on all three charges.

OPENING STATEMENT

May it please the Court, Craig Dilger, Judge Schoering, ladies and gentlemen of the jury. Drugs, guns, cellular phones, outstanding arrest warrants, suspended licenses, and numerous other traffic violations. I'll go over that again. Drugs, crack cocaine, marijuana, guns, 9mm semiautomatic weapons, outstanding arrest warrants, suspended licenses, and other traffic violations.

Now you might say what does that have to do with the case that is about stolen vehicle, stolen vehicle parts, and theft by deception? Those are the things that were found in the cars when they were stopped by the police. Frederick Dorsey, Timothy Belmar, Lorenzo Curry, Don French, Tyrone Bunzy, and James Sheckles. Those are the things found with those individuals in those cars. The defendant was not found in any car. You are not going to have any witness, other than the people that alleged he rented the cars to them, come in and say they saw the defendant in a car. You are not going to have any witness, no police officer and no employee of Avis Rent A Car say they saw the defendant in an Avis vehicle.

Now you do have Juan Williams' mother, who is a late midnight hour, 11th hour conversion witness. I only found out about it this morning. The Commonwealth only found out about it yesterday. She now has some information that she wants to come forward with. Well it's obvious why she would come in, to help her son, who by the way is a convicted felon.

What else is there about these names? Now during voir dire Mr. Dilger named nine witnesses. Now he says there are only three witnesses. So we went from nine to three. Where are the other six people?

Also, and what he didn't tell you, but what I will tell you is that Mr. Belmar was arrested and charged with receiving stolen property over $300 for the car that he was driving. That charge was dismissed. Mr. Bunzy was arrested and charged with receiving stolen property over $300. His charge was dismissed. Mr. Dorsey was charged with theft by unlawful taking of an automobile-- dismissed. Mr. French, theft by unlawful taking of an automobile--dismissed. The convicted felon, Juan Williams, receiving stolen property over $300, and the one with the 9 mm, his charges--dismissed.

They have no fingerprints from any of the defendant in any of those cars. They found no property, no identification, or property of any sort, or any other articles belonging to the defendant. A lot of times when police go out and they make an arrest, and they think they have solved a case they are so sure they are right, they stop their investigation and that's what happened in this case. Sometimes when it looks as if they are wrong, they are unable to back away and say we made a mistake. Craig Dilger indicated they were going to show you "control or possession." I want you to keep those in mind because that is part of the statute on possession. I want you to test the evidence by that little line, control or possession of two more vehicles at one time.

Well he also said it's easy for employees to get the cars out of the lot. Well it's easy because Avis has a lack of security. I don't know about the other car rental agencies. I seldom rent a car because I have a car. But most places you go, I went to Mobile Alabama last week and we flew to New Orleans, and we rented a car. Before you drive out of the car lot, there is a little guard shack there and you hand the papers to the man, and he checks to make sure you got the right car. It's not done at Avis. Anybody can walk on the lot 24 hours a day. Even the police report, which you will have, will show you that there are two or more sets of keys to any one of these cars.

There is basically an open door policy, anybody can walk on the lot at any hour of the day, and take a car. You can go in and rent a car, come out and get in the wrong, car and drive away. There is no security and no control. What we ask you to do in this case is to look at all the evidence. You said you would keep an open mind. We ask you to look at each witness as they come in. What is their motive to testify and what are they getting in exchange for their testimony? When you look at this entire case, I am sure and convinced that at the end of this case, you will have a reasonable doubt and you will return a verdict of not guilty for my client.

CLOSING ARGUMENT

May it please the Court, Judge Schoering, Mr. Dilger, ladies and gentlemen of the jury, this is the part of the trial at which your duty begins, and our duty kind of ends. First of all let me say, since I am an officer of the Court, thanks on behalf of myself and my client, for your attention, your attentiveness, and your service here.

As jurors you perform a very important service to the Commonwealth by serving as jurors. This is the best system that our country has for deciding a person's guilt or innocence. It is an old system, but it's the best we have. And we use it, and sometimes we take what jurors do lightly. But we want to say thank you for your service.

As I indicated your job is now beginning. Most stories have one beginning and one end. This one has two beginnings and two endings, because after I stand up, and Mr. Dilger stands up, and then you go and do your duty.

And your task is a simple task, but it is a very serious and solemn task. When you swear, when you take the oath, you swear that you will do justice in this case. You will do the right thing in this particular case. We are not talking or looking at any other case. We are just looking at this case and this defendant who's on trial here, the defendant.

Under our system the Commonwealth gets the last word. So it's important you listen to what I say. Once I sit down, I can't get back up. It's not like when we are questioning, and he will question, and I will question, and then we can go back a couple or more times. We can't do that in closing. I get to say mine, he gets to say his, and you get to decide the case.

At the beginning of the case we asked you whether you understood certain things. We asked you whether you understood that the indictment, even though it was read and might be read to you again, the indictment is not evidence, and cannot be considered as evidence. You said you understood that.

We also asked you whether you understood that the presumption of innocence comes into the courtroom with this defendant, and follows this defendant throughout the trial. He is presumed to be innocent until you go back and deliberate and return with a verdict. You said you understood that.

You also said you understood and could be fair and decide this case, not based on sympathy, bias, or prejudice; but This book is but decide this case based on two things; the testimony that came from the witness stand, and the other thing that you have to use is your common sense to decide this case.

Now the Commonwealth made you some promises at the beginning of this case. Some promises I believe that were not kept, and I want to remind you of some of those.

The Commonwealth promised you they would bring in eight or nine witnesses. They read a list, but some of those witnesses, as we know now, are missing. They didn't come in here to the courtroom and testify.

Specifically, James Sheckles, who was arrested in one of the cars that was stolen, Timothy Belmar, who was arrested in one of the cars, and Frederick Dorsey, who was arrested in the first car. They didn't bring in any of those people. They didn't bring in any of those witnesses. Why did they promise that to you and not live up to their promise?

Mr. Dilger also said he would show you or as he said, "It is illegal in the Commonwealth of KY to be in control or possession of two or more stolen cars at one time." Now I ask you, did they show you that the defendant was ever in control or possession of two or more cars at one time?

I will put this back [*Hagan referring to chart*] because this morning they brought in Mr. Weller, again from the Avis car rental, but what did he say? He said that one car was taken on August 18th. Another car was taken on August the 2nd, and the third car was taken sometime later in August. But it still does not show that he was in control or possession of two of those three cars at any one time.

Now which two? Was he in possession of this one and this one, or this one, or this one, or these two? Now you have to make a guessing game. Only from the witness stand do you know who was in possession or control of these vehicles, all of the people that were arrested in these vehicles, all of the people that were charged with receiving stolen property, or charged with theft by unlawful taking.

All of the people that had their cases dismissed in District Court, and a couple in juvenile court. Those were the people that were caught with their hands in the cookie jar. And when they get caught, they want to blame it on someone else, someone that they know that works there.

Well you might say "how did they get these cars"? Well remember, we don't have any burden. That's not our burden to figure out how they got these cars. The Commonwealth has the only burden in this case, and the burden is to convince you beyond a reasonable doubt that he took the cars. And I believe that doubt is lacking in this case.

Now we didn't have all of the police officers to come in. We had a couple to come in this morning, and all they could say was which cars they stopped and which people they arrested. Nowhere did any of the three witnesses that the Commonwealth put on say anything about whether the car they were in had a Budget sticker on it, or which car it was from Budget. I'm sorry, not Budget, Avis, which car it was from Avis?

This case really boils down to three witnesses. It doesn't boil down to Detective Cox, even though he did a fine job. He did the job what he was supposed to do, okay. It doesn't boil down to the man from Avis Rent A Car, Mr. Weller. He reported the thefts, and with the cooperation of the police, they finally put everything together and charged this defendant. But neither of these gentlemen saw the defendant in possession of a car. Neither gentlemen saw him in possession of a car.

Pamela Williams, this lady that came in with this midnight conversion, a last minute story. She didn't see the defendant in possession of a car. The only people that say he was in possession of a car were the people that were caught in the cars.

How did they know he worked there? He worked there because he came back to River City Corrections and had on a uniform. That's how they knew he worked there. Stories were changing. They were skillfully omitting some things, and remembering some things they wanted to remember.

Don French, who I believe was their first witness, was the gentlemen that sat there in the chair, and kind of kept his eyes closed. I looked down and asked him a question? He kind of paused and took a half minute or minute to answer a question.

Mr. Dilger's first question? Do you remember July 28 of last year 1995? Yes. Did you speak with the defendant on that day? Well, I am not sure. I guess so. I can't remember exactly which day. Now if he says it was the 28th and these cars were only taken in August, then what car is he referring to? Did you speak with the defendant on the telephone on the 28th? I can't remember exactly.

Now you can remember the testimony for yourself, or if you want to you can get the videotape and take it back to the room, and ask for the tape to be replayed.

Then we asked him about the amount. Well I think it was $150.00. Then I think it was $100.00. He didn't know the amount, he didn't know the date.

He said it was in the summer months and then I asked him? Well, do you know which months in the summer? Well whatever the summer months are, June July or August. I said, well can you be a little more specific? He says, "I can't remember the exact day."

I asked him about the time of day? Well, be a little more specific. He says, "well between three and five, and then he changed it into six or seven.

And then I said, well is there anything, anything else? He said, "well it was getting dark Well anybody of any age and any intelligence knows that in the summer time it is not dark at 6 or 7 clock.

I asked him about the charges? What happened to the charges? I guess they got dismissed. Now, ladies and gentlemen, you would know if you were arrested for something and whether they got dismissed, wouldn't be any guessing game. You would know whether those charges were pending, or whether you pled guilty, or whether they got dismissed.

Then we asked him how familiar were you were with the defendant? Well earlier Mr. Dilger asked him was he a friend? I think it was the second or third question. He said, "well yes we were friends." But I asked him, did you ever go to his house? No. Ever play basketball together? No. Did you know where he lived? No. Well how long have you been familiar with him? Well I guess we've been familiar with him I guess since we started getting cars.

Now who is trying to fool in saying he that he was a friend of the defendant? If he didn't know him before, didn't know where he lived, didn't know where he worked, didn't go out with him, and didn't play ball or anything with him like that? Who is he trying to fool in saying that he's a friend of the defendant?

The next witness that they brought in was, Juan Williams, the guy that had on the little orange shirt sitting there. He also considered him a friend. He didn't go out with him, didn't play ball together. He kind of knew him through his grandmother, or knew him through his sister. He was the one that said, "I came to the defendant, he didn't ask me, I asked him"

Now how could he be deceived if he was the one asking about renting a car, knowing that he didn't have any of the things that are required in most communities for renting a car, a credit card, a phone in your name, employment, and a valid operator's license?

And then I asked him, did anything unusual happen in the car? And he said no. But then I corrected him, and I said, well didn't you get arrested with a 9mm? "Oh it was in the car, but it wasn't mine "

Well ladies and gentlemen, if it wasn't his, why did he go downstairs, which he admitted on the stand, in District Court, and plead guilty to carrying a concealed deadly weapon, that 9mm?

Now he wasn't sure about the date either. He said it was in August. I am not sure, but I think it was in August. And I asked him about insurance. "Oh well, I wasn't really worried about insurance." He didn't know where the defendant lived.

The police officers in this case arrested five, six, or seven people. And we've heard names today that we didn't even know of yesterday, another juvenile today that wasn't even mentioned yesterday. The police officers did all they could do and all of these stories continued to change.

One guy says I got the car from Donnie. Then Donnie says I got it from the defendant. Tyrone says he told my friends about it, and that's how I got it. I connected it up through my friend.

Ladies and gentlemen, I say to you that these witnesses are not believable. If they would lie about one thing, they would lie about another. And I ask you to completely disregard their testimony.

To convict somebody and send them to the penitentiary, you need truthful and credible evidence that comes from witnesses that don't have a motive to lie, that don't have a motive to change their story, that don't have a motive to change dates or conveniently forget dates.

They are forgetting dates. They are forgetting times. They are forgetting places. They are forgetting amounts, all of the critical things you need to decide this case. All of these witnesses seem to forget. They can't forget they were arrested because we have the police officers who know they were arrested. They can't forget that.

Now, I'd like you to try to figure out this car who got it and when? Who did they get this car from and where did they get it from? How long was it gone? In order for you to find him guilty of theft by deception over $300, as these Instructions give you the opportunity to do, it says if and only if you believe from the evidence beyond a reasonable doubt that on or about the 9th day of June...

Have you heard any testimony about June the 9th in reference to these three cars? Remember we are not talking about any other cars. We are talking about these three. Has there been any testimony about June, or any testimony about July. These cars were taken in August, according to Mr. Weller.

And now when you get to the money portion of this, [*reading from Instructions*]...that he deceived Avis of over $300.00.

Well how much for this car? They say the average rate is $37.00 a day. Is that a weekday rate? The weekend rate is usually lower. Discounts apply all over the place. If you are triple AAA member you get a discount. If you are a member of the bar association, you get another discount. If you have one of these Avis Passport Gold cards, it may give you another discount. There are all kinds of discounts out there. So if you can't figure out which amount applies, how are you going to figure out that it totals $300?

Now as to trafficking in stolen vehicles, [*Hagan reading instruction*] You can find the defendant guilty or not guilty under this instruction, only if you believe from the evidence, now again, beyond a reasonable doubt...

And let me say a word about beyond a reasonable doubt. That's the compass that has to guide your deliberations. And the judge over here in the Instructions explains it even more and says, that if upon the whole case you have a reasonable doubt that the defendant is guilty, you shall find him not guilty

If upon the whole case... If you look at this whole case, and try to put everything together that we have from the witness stand, not things that didn't come in, just from the witness stand. If upon the whole case you have a reasonable doubt, you shall find him not guilty. Shall is a mandatory word. You shall find him not guilty. If you look at this whole case, and it springs reasonable doubts up in your mind, then look at those doubts; point those doubts out to your fellow jurors. Let them know where you have doubt at in this case.

And you heard several of the gentlemen that got up there were convicted felons. One is going up for parole in January. Don't you think he expects some favorable testimony for coming in here and testifying? They've already got charges dismissed against all of them.

Mr. Weller also said that he looked at the film, the film from the cameras that are all around Standiford Field. He couldn't see the defendant doing anything unusual, didn't even see him on the film. He also said no employees told him the defendant was behind the desk, doing what he wasn't supposed to do, or coming to get keys for which he was not authorized. Nor did anybody mention to him that the defendant was gone away from his station or his place of work for an extended period of time that would cause some concern.

Now if he was taking this many cars on and off during this period of time, don't you think that somebody would have noticed him for being missing for an hour, and half-hour? Where is the defendant? I wonder where he is. He's been gone an half an hour, he's been gone an hour.

Of course if we knew when and where, we might be able to determine who did what, and which cars were taken on what dates, and the amounts of those rentals. Mr. Weller wasn't even asked how much did Avis lose as a result of this.

We don't know if they lost a $100 or $150.00 or some other sum. We don't know. That question wasn't even asked.
What they want you to do is to guess. They want you to say, "Well $37.00 a day, and this car was gone for X number of days, and this car was gone for X number of days." They want you to kind of just guesswork. Were not here about guesswork, were not here for hunches. We are not here for suspicions.

It's not enough for them to paint a picture that he's probably guilty, he's possible guilty, or that these cars couldn't have been taken by anybody else, or it couldn't have happened any other way.

They have got to prove to you that he is guilty beyond a reasonable doubt. Each and every one of you twelve that will decide this case has to be convinced beyond a reasonable doubt. Now let the Commonwealth explain to you why they didn't bring the juveniles in. Tyrone Williams--who was arrested with his brother. Let them explain why they didn't bring the other juvenile in who was arrested. Let them explain the whereabouts of the person with the first car.

You know the first one is probably more critical than the last one, because if we brought that person in, we might know when this all started. Can you really tell from just these cars when this all started? I know they've got a date in here of June, but there has been no testimony about June.

Ladies and gentlemen the Commonwealth would have you believe that most of the people were deceived? That's a lot of blue smoke. At least two of them said, "Well I knew I was underage and knew I couldn't rent a car." So how could they think they were renting a legitimate leased vehicle from an authorized agent of Avis, if they knew they were underage, knew they didn't have a valid license, some of them with suspended licenses. How could they think they were deceived? No, they are trying to deceive you.

They are trying to deceive you in believing, "we've done our part downstairs, and now we are up here, if we do our part it's all over, our cases are already dismissed" Would we have had their testimony if their charges had not been dismissed?

I would submit to you ladies and gentlemen that you don't need a lot of reasonable doubt in this case. You just need one single solitary reasonable doubt in this case to find this defendant not guilty of all of these charges. I do not believe that the Commonwealth has painted the complete picture for you.

I thought we would get a board up here that kind of said when all the cars were taken, when they were recovered, the amount of the daily rental rates, the amount of the loss to Avis. But we don't have that, not from the evidence. But he might do that when he gets up in closing. Remember closing is not evidence. This is just our summary of the evidence. You've got to look at the evidence alone that came out of that witness chair.

And when you look at the evidence in this case, it boils down to three people that are so unbelievable I don't even believe Shakespeare could describe them. You have got to look at those three witnesses, and say to this man you are going to the penitentiary based on what those three want to be credible witnesses said on the stand. One of them couldn't even look you in the eye. Another kept waving his hat as he was testifying.

I would ask you go back to that jury room go back and take your time. Take all the time that it takes. I know this is Sweet Sixteen day and both the University of Kentucky and University of Louisville [*Hagan referring to NCAA games later that night involving local teams*] are going to play tonight, and everybody wants to get home and watch them, and I do too. But if I have to miss those games because you are deliberating, so be it. I ask you to take all the time that is necessary, don't think that because this case didn't have twenty or thirty witnesses, or twenty or thirty exhibits that it is not an important case.

When you look back at your decision later, you will hopefully say to yourself, "I know I did the right thing." And as we indicated to you in the beginning, if you tell the prosecutor you have not proven your case beyond a reasonable doubt, you are still following the law.

And I would ask you to go back to that jury room and return a verdict of not guilty on all charges in this case. Thank you very much.

CASE #6

Date of verdict:	June 26, 1997
Charge:	Theft by Unlawful Taking over $300, Class D Felony
Possible sentence:	1 to 5 years
Judge:	Hon. Kenneth Conliffe, Jefferson Circuit Court
Prosecutor:	Hon. Chad Elder
Defendants opening statement:	3 minutes
Defendant's closing argument:	11 minutes
Commonwealth's closing argument:	17 minutes
Reasonable Doubt used	11 times
Length of jury deliberations:	2 hrs 18 minutes
Was defendant a convicted felon?	NO
Did defendant testify?	NO
Verdict:	**NOT GUILTY**

SYNOPSIS

The defendant was an employee of the City of Louisville and worked in the Solid Waste Division. A $3,000 Bunton lawnmower owned by the City came up missing. Several employees said that the defendant unloaded the lawnmower at his mother's house. The defendant and two other city employees were fired.

After the employees were fired, they began talking and ended up getting their jobs back. An investigation revealed that several of the employees said that the defendant stole the lawnmower and told them to keep quiet about it. The defendant was charged with one count of theft by unlawful taking over $300.00

The jury returned a verdict of **NOT GUILTY** on the charge of Theft by Unlawful Taking over $300.00.

OPENING STATEMENT

Judge Conliffe, Mr. Dilger, ladies and gentlemen of the jury. There are two sides to every story. You will hear those two sides today. I will ask you, as I asked you in voir dire, don't be swayed by who goes first. The Commonwealth, according to our system of justice, always goes first in a criminal case. Don't be swayed by who has the most witnesses. What I want you to look at is the witness's motive to testify truthfully, or to cloud that testimony.

Charles Brame, he gets fired for this theft or this alleged theft and he doesn't say anything for five months. He's off and he decides the defendant stole it. He goes back and says the defendant did it and he gets his job back. Terry Patterson, he is part-time at the time of the theft of the lawnmower, he doesn't say anything. Several months go by and what's his reward for talking. He's now full time for the city of Louisville. Those are the kind of witnesses that you are going to hear from. I want you to remember something. We are talking about a lawnmower that weighs over 300 pounds that one person could not possibly pick up and take off of that truck by themselves. My client says he didn't take any lawnmower off of the city of Louisville truck. He's been employed by the city of Louisville for six years. Now if he wanted to take something, he is a driver. He certainly had plenty of opportunities to take something. He's been employed there six years. He's never been involved with a theft. The driver is ultimately responsible, because he's the one that's driving. He's the one that has the key. These other guys, I don't know even if they have a driver's license or can drive. So if something comes up missing, you look to the lead person on the crew.

What I want you to concentrate on is the date or the dates they say this lawnmower was taken. You are going to hear May 29th. You are going to hear June 3. You are going to hear May 3rd. You are going to hear the week of May 3rd. And then for some strange reason, it is not until August that this detective takes out a warrant against my client for the theft of this mower. Why would it tale over two months and why was this incident not even reported until June 20th?

Now what happened in between May 29th and June 20th is crucial because you would think that if these guys are still working for the city of Louisville, how can they do their job if they don't have a mower on the truck? They are still employed there. I will ask you to look at all of those things. I ask you to look at the location from which it was taken. My client will tell you why he stopped at 4908 Primrose Way, where his mother lives. I will also ask you to look at the city of

Louisville's, I guess you want to say, their equipment inventory or their system for keeping up with equipment. We don't believe that they can show you or that they will show you, and the evidence will be, that they don't know what equipment is on what truck, when it was last there, who used it, when its checked back in, when its checked back out. No inventory control system whatsoever so you can track whether a particular piece of equipment has come up missing, and who is the last person to use it. Certainly if you knew who the last person was that used it, you could go to that person. My client doesn't even know what particular day it was on that truck, because some days the crew goes out without a mower. Some days they have weed eaters, rakes, shovels, and they are merely cleaning up lots and they are bundling up old equipment old mattresses, or whatever is on junk lots. They are not mowing everyday. I ask you to listen to all of the evidence, and if the Commonwealth does not paint the complete or full picture for you, at the end of the case, I'll be back up here, and I will be asking you to return a verdict of not guilty. Thank you.

CLOSING ARGUMENT

May it please the Court, Judge Conliffe, Mr. Elder, ladies and gentlemen of the jury. First of all, on behalf of my client, let me thank you for your service. What you do as jurors is much appreciated. It is the only system known in the world that has worked for as long as it has. It is the only way we have to determine guilt or innocence under our criminal justice system.

As Mr. Elder has said, "the criminal trial is a search for the truth." And this is where my job ends, the judge's job ends, Mr. Elder's job ends, and your job begins. You are here to determine what happened on or about June 3, 1996 in this particular case. Not in any other case, but this particular case.

The judge has read the Instructions to you, and I won't go over them all, but I will go over Instruction No.3, and that's very important. [*Hagan reading reasonable doubt instruction*] You shall find, you shall, you shall find the defendant not guilty unless you are satisfied from the evidence alone, from what came from that witness chair, and beyond a reasonable doubt that he is guilty.

No two ways about it. You shall find the defendant not guilty, unless you are satisfied from the evidence alone, and beyond a reasonable doubt that he is guilty... Not from, "well he must be guilty or he would not be here" That's not good enough. Not from "well if he didn't do it, who did it"? That's not evidence beyond a reasonable doubt, but from the evidence alone that has been presented to you.

If upon the whole case, if after you look at this whole set of circumstances, all the witnesses that have been put on by the Commonwealth, and the one witness that we put on. If upon the whole case you have a reasonable doubt that he is guilty, these Instructions say you shall find him not guilty.

I would submit to you that in this case the Commonwealth has not painted the full picture. It is not your job to determine who stole a lawnmower from the city of Louisville on or about June 3. Your job is simply to determine, if from the evidence that's been presented in this courtroom over the last few days, the Commonwealth has satisfied its burden of proving to you beyond a reasonable doubt that it was this defendant that took that particular lawnmower.

And we are not talking about any other theft on any other occasion. They are mentioning a Bunton lawnmower, that was a 32 inch cut with 14 horsepower, with a certain model number, and a certain serial number.

I would submit to you that this is not a complex case. It's pretty simple, because when you pull away the last four witnesses,

Detective Alpieger, Mr. Reed, Mr. Chapman, Mr. Huddleston, none of them can tell you that they saw anyone with a Bunton lawnmower, or saw anyone take a Bunton lawnmower.

Detective Alpieger, and it is not his fault that he was given the case in August, after it lay dormant over there in the Fifth District for two months. He goes and gets it, and he just interviews a couple people, and takes out a warrant against the defendant for the theft of a lawnmower, because that's who Charles Brame said stole the lawnmower.

But don't you think if he was doing a thorough investigation, he would investigate, interview, or attempt to interview the one person that they said took the lawnmower. He didn't.

And Mr. Reed, he doesn't shed much light. He's from the Bunton Company. It's pretty good equipment, a 32 inch cut. But what did he tell you that is going to help you decide this case--nothing.

And Mr. Chapman, he may be more unbelievable than Mr. Patterson or Mr. Brame. Because Mr. Chapman wants us to believe that the serial # here is from the lawnmower that was taken. But we know that the serial # given on the police report is a different serial number. No, Mr. Hagan you've got that wrong. No, the model number was under it. Sn usually means serial number.

But which lawnmower are we talking about being taken on June 3. I don't know, and I would submit that there is not evidence beyond a reasonable doubt that this defendant took one of these two lawnmowers on that particular day.

And then, Mr. Huddleston, now he says that the lawnmower had no tires, and that one lawnmower was in the shop. Well another witness came in and said, "well, two lawnmowers would not fit in that truck." And if one lawnmower was in the shop, and this one had no tires, why would you ride around all of this time with a lawnmower that is not working? He said he's been there six years, and he's never used that lawnmower.

Then we come to a couple of witnesses that even *Shakespeare* couldn't describe, Charles Brame and Terry Patterson. Charles Brame says he only got a midnight conversion when the police showed up at his door. And then even when the police showed up at his door, he did not tell the truth. I didn't want to get involved. The only reason I am here today is I because got a subpoena. If I didn't get a subpoena, I wouldn't be here.

Now that's the witness that the Commonwealth wants you to use, to believe that the defendant took the lawnmower, and send him to the penitentiary. That witness, who said he lied for five months, and then covered it up. Who I asked, "Well did you resign or get fired." He said, "Oh no, I got fired." Then I showed him his statement that he signed on August 7, and had him to read it. Resignation, I want all my money that the city owes me. But for some mysterious reason beyond that point, he gets his job back, and not only does he get his job back, but Terry Patterson is promoted to full time.

It is yours to determine the credibility of every witness that comes before you. There are some things in this case that I will draw your attention to, and let Mr. Elder answer these questions, and whether they raise reasonable doubt.

The Commonwealth read to you a list of witnesses. Gary Chapman, Terry Patterson, Charles Brame. And then they read Leonard Butler. Where was Mr. Butler and why didn't he come in and testify? They promised you that he would.

Did any witness come and say that the defendant took a lawnmower on a specific date, or around a specific date? Charles Brame couldn't remember any date. He doesn't know what month it was that he stopped over his mother's house. Mr. Patterson couldn't remember a date. Even Mr. Huddleston got so confused that he said, "Well, Terry talked about it in May." Well, but his statement says he talked about it in June? How then did he talk to him about it in May?

Did anyone ever conduct a search of the city's inventory to determine if both of these lawnmowers were there, or if one may have been in the shop? My client says it was in the shop for over a year.

And then there was a report that a lawnmower was unloaded in the 4500 block of Winrose Way. His mother is not the only one that lives on Winrose Way and that has a connection to the city. Charles Huddleston lives on Winrose Way. Did anybody ever go in his yard and look and see if there was a lawnmower there?

And then Terry Patterson comes in, and Mr. Elder asks him the question? Did anybody say anything to you while you were in the truck or before you left? No. And then I asked him the same question at first. And then I showed him his statement. He says, "We were told if anybody asked us, we don't know anything."

Ladies and gentlemen, who is he trying to fool? Whose eyes is he trying to pull the wool over? He lied before, he lied now. Charles Brame lied for five months. He was lying yesterday about this lawnmower. For some reason when they decide to come clean and shift the blame to the driver, for some mysterious reason, they get their jobs back.

Mr. Elder said at the beginning, he conceded to you, that they were not going to come in here with clean hands. I would submit to you that not only were their hands not clean, they were outright liars.

And he said that Charles Brame wants to claim willful ignorance and that's fine. No, that's not fine because this gentleman is facing five years in the penitentiary. No, that's not fine.

And I asked either one of them, did you ever tell your supervisor on the next day that he took a lawnmower off the truck?

No. I asked Mr. Patterson and he said, "he first didn't know really know the policy." He said, "oh yes the policy was thoroughly, he used the word thoroughly, explained to us." Did you ever tell your supervisor on June 4th, June 2nd, or June 5th that a lawnmower had been taken? No.

And then we get this line about somebody started dropping hints I believe that the ones that dropped the hints were the ones that took the lawnmower.

Yes Mr. Elder is right. The criminal trial is a search for the truth. I used to wonder why my great-grandmother used to tell me that a liar is worse than a thief.

I think it was *George Herbert* that said, *"Show me a liar, and I'll show you the thief."* And it was *Pope* that said, *"He who tells a lie is not sensible how great a task he undertakes, because he must be forced to invent 20 more to maintain that one."*

I would submit to you that both of those gentlemen were liars. They were lying before now, and they were lying yesterday, and they are trying to continue to cover it up as to who took this lawnmower.

Remember, it's not our burden to go out here and to determine for you who actually took the lawnmower. It is merely your job to determine whether the Commonwealth, through its witnesses, they called those witnesses, proved their case to you beyond a reasonable doubt.

And when you go back to the jury room if you have doubts about this case, I want you to express the doubts that you have to the other jurors; whether it comes from something I said, or from the witness chair, or whether it comes from something you picked up on your own. Express those doubts to your fellow jurors.

And when you go back there, I believe I said at the beginning of the case, this is not one of those sensational headline grabbing cases. No television cameras are going to be here, but this case is still important to this defendant. His life and liberty are both at stake. He wants his job back. He intends to get his job back.

Stay back there all day if necessary to do what is right, and do not compromise with what is wrong. Thank you ladies and gentlemen.

CASE #7

Date of verdict: March 12, 1998

Charge: Murder, Capital Offense
Possible Sentence: 20 to 50 years or Life, or Life without parole for 25 years

Judge: Hon. Thomas Wine
Jefferson Circuit Court

Prosecutors: Hon. John Balliet &
Hon. Sheila Waxman

Defendants opening argument: 10 minutes
Commonwealth's closing argument: 12 minutes
Defendant's closing argument: 30 minutes
Reasonable Doubt used 33 times
Length of jury deliberations: 20 to 25 minutes

Was defendant a convicted felon? YES
Did defendant testify? NO

Verdict: **NOT GUILTY**

SYNOPSIS

The defendant was charged with a single count of Murder for the death of Stephan Rudolph. His girlfriend gave a party for his birthday. The victim was an uninvited guest who, along with some of his friends, decided to crash the party. He flashed a weapon and started a disruption. After being asked to leave, he flipped tables over on the way out. He was shot as he crossed the street in front of the West End Lions Club.

Neighbors testified to hearing lots of gunshots and the only witness to accuse the defendant of shooting Mr. Rudolph was a friend of his. However, the witness was nearly a block away when it happened. The street was dark and his view was blocked by some trees. Police never found the murder weapon and never charged anyone else, even though at least three other people had guns in the party and came outside and started shooting. There were projectiles fond at the scene that indicated the presence of at least three or four different calibers of weapons.

Many of the persons at the party were never interviewed or talked to by the police, and none of the persons were tested for gunshot residue.

The Judge gave the jury Instructions on murder, manslaughter and reckless homicide. The defendant did not testify. After deliberating less than twenty five minutes, the jury returned a **NOT GUILTY** verdict as to all charges.

OPENING STATEMENT

May it please the Court, Judge Wine, Mr. Balliet, Ms. Waxman, Detective Finch, fellow counsel, ladies and gentlemen of the jury. When people differ in their versions of an incident, many questions often go unanswered.

But today you as a jury will attempt to determine the facts, and whether the Commonwealth can meet its burden of establishing beyond a reasonable doubt that this man killed Stephon Rudolph on May 17, 1997.

Have you ever taken a car trip and before you get in your car, you go to AAA and get them to route your trip, or you pull out an old map and find out which direction to go in?

Well an opening argument or opening statement is similar. The purpose is to provide you a **roadmap** to help you follow the evidence in the trial, as it comes in, and to hopefully place that evidence in its proper context. The evidence will come from the witness stand and the law will come from His Honor, Judge Wine, at the end of the case.

I would like for you to remember several things. One is that there are two sides to every story. And second, please look at both the motive of each witness to testify, and the character and credibility of each of those witnesses.

Once you look at the evidence here, what you will find is that there are several things missing and something terribly wrong with this evidence. You'll find an incomplete investigation. Witnesses were not talked to or interviewed. Leads are not followed in the critical forty-eight hours after the death of Stephon Rudolph.

A lot of tests were not done that could have been done. The police, as they often are, were hampered in their search for the truth, by witnesses that didn't see anything and didn't want to be involved, because of fear or other reasons. Let's see what the evidence will show as it relates to the defendant.

Now let's just look at the facts. Once the police arrived, they were told that at one time or another at least twenty or thirty people were at the party. Yet the evidence will show that, even today, many of these witnesses have never been contacted. Many have never been asked to give a written or recorded statement.

You'll find that statements were taken from witnesses even after this defendant was indicted, arrested, and arraigned in this Court. The evidence will also be that the police never found the murder weapon. They don't know which caliber of weapon was used to kill Mr. Rudolph. And the evidence will be that they found four different shell casings from three different calibers of weapons; a 25-caliber shell, a 32-caliber shell, and a 9mm caliber shell.

They were so sure they had solved this crime, the evidence will show, that they stopped their investigation, and failed to follow up on some leads which would have really solved this crime.

The police jumped to the wrong conclusion, and will never face their mistake, and admit they were wrong, or just don't know who shot and killed Stephon Rudolph.

FACT #1

There is not and will be no evidence in this case that anyone, on the night of this homicide, said that Charles Russell had a weapon or fired a weapon.

FACT #2

Charles Russell has never made a statement saying that he had a weapon or fired a weapon.

FACT #3

And the testimony of the only two people that said Charles was shooting came from one of them three weeks afterwards, and the other almost four months after it happened.

FACT #4

There will not be credible evidence as to how many people were shooting out there that night.

FACT #5

And there will be no evidence as to which shot hit Mr. Rudolph, and as to which way he was facing. Evidence will be that he was pretty intoxicated, a .213 on the breathalyzer test. So he was pretty intoxicated, and the evidence will be that he was inside the party, busting balloons, pulling down decorations, and flipping over tables. And then he is asked to leave. And as he and his buddies are going out the door, he gets in the middle of the street cursing, hollering, screaming, and throwing gang signs.

FACT #6

And then the evidence will be from their witness, one of several people they took a recorded statement from, that one of his buddies fired the first shot. And the evidence will be that not only one but ten, fifteen, twenty, who knows how many shots, were fired?

It's not our job to solve this crime. The judge will tell you and the law says that it's their job. In the end, we do not believe there is one shred of credible evidence, which will convince you beyond a reasonable doubt that my client, Charles Russell, shot and killed Stephon Rudolph. I don't believe you can or will render a guilty verdict on this type of evidence.

CLOSING ARGUMENT

Once again, may it please the Court, Mr. Balliet, Ms. Waxman, the defendant's family, the Rudolph family, ladies and gentlemen of the jury. On behalf of myself and my client, the defendant, I would like to thank each of you, each one of the twelve of you. Sometimes we take it for granted what a valuable service you as jurors provide. But I'd like to thank each of you for your service as jurors.

I'd also like to apologize as to something I said during opening argument. I might have misstated that when the police got there, they talked to Stephan Rudolph. No, they did not talk to Stephan Rudolph. What I meant was the police talked to Henry Crawford and that's whose truck it was.

Now most stories have one beginning and one end. This trial has two beginning and two endings, because my job as defense counsel, and Mr. Balliet's job as prosecutor is about to end. And your job, as jurors, or the conscience of the community, is about to begin.

I pointed out to you in opening that your task in this case is simple, to be fair and to do justice, to do the right thing in this case. At the beginning of this case when we questioned you, we asked you whether you understood certain things.

One was that the burden of proof is always on the Commonwealth. The burden is never on the defendant. We don't have to prove anything. The burden always has been, still is, and always will be on the Commonwealth.

We also asked you whether you understood, and I believe you said you did, that the defendant walks into this courtroom with the presumption of innocence. And that presumption stays with him throughout the trial until you go back and deliberate and return a verdict.

We also asked you whether you could decide this thing, decide this case based on two things; not on sympathy and not on emotion, but on two things; the evidence and the facts that come from this chair [*Hagan touching witness chair*] right here, and the Instructions of law as the Court just read to you. And we will go over those Instructions a little bit later.

Finally you said that you understood and that you could follow the law as to the amount of proof necessary for the Commonwealth to convict the defendant of the charge of murder. And now we have these other or two lesser included offenses. But you said you understood that, and the judge told you that was the highest burden, proof beyond a reasonable doubt, as to each and every element of each of these offenses.

So when you go back there and take these Instructions and Instruction #6 has that Instruction in there. You might just want to write, so you don't forget it, you might just want to write over the Instruction on intentional murder, reasonable doubt still applies. It still applies as to wanton murder. It still applies as to manslaughter in the 2nd degree, and it still applies as to reckless homicide. It still has to be beyond a reasonable doubt.

And we told you that the Commonwealth alone, with no help from the defendant, has to paint the complete picture. And if they don't paint that picture for you, you are still upholding the law when you look Mr. Balliet in the eye and tell him, "you have not proven your case beyond a reasonable doubt." You are still following the law.

And during my opening, I told you that we would show you that there were a lot of shots fired. People were firing in different directions. Several shooters, a number of different shell casings from a number of different weapons. I believe we kept our promises.

Now I took notes during the Commonwealth's Opening, and they also made some promises. Mr. Balliet said the focus should not be on these sub- issues, but on who fired the gun and who is telling the truth.

And he also said that as the party proceeded, people became rowdier Yes they did, and who became rowdier? That was Stephan Rudolph, and some other of the friends that were with him, and we know from witness testimony that Antonio Sublet may have become rowdier, so rowdier that he pulled a gun out.

It is obvious that the Commonwealth has defaulted on its promises as far as this defendant is concerned. They gave you a promise, and instead of honoring that promise, and keeping that commitment, they have given you a bad check, a check that has come back marked insufficient evidence.

The writer *James Baldwin* once said, "*The moment we break faith with one another or with our promises, the sea engulfs us, the lights go out.*" And I believe that the light has gone out on the Commonwealth, as far as this defendant is concerned, as far as this case is concerned.

Now for some reason the police said a few days after the murder they suspected that the defendant was the shooter. Ladies and gentlemen, suspicion is not proof, suspicion is not proof.

And you heard from one of their witnesses, the lady that did the gunshot residue test whose name was on there as a suspect? Derrick Powell. He was also suspected. He's not on trial here for murder. The defendant is the only one.

You heard that Lamont Bruno Brown fired a gun and fired first. He's not on trial here for murder. You heard from both Nicole and from Tim Howard that said Antonio Sublet had a gun He's not on trial here for murder, only the defendant. It's his birthday party and he's a convenient scapegoat.

You know it's like going to the race track and trying to pick one of those horses out, just pick one and move on. That's not enough to prove this case, that's not enough to prove this case. This is not a one horse race. The Commonwealth wants you to send this man to the penitentiary on the evidence that they presented to you.

Now what do we know about Antonio Sublet? And when you all boil it down, Ms. Leola Murphy she doesn't know who did the shooting. The coroner doesn't know who did the shooting. The lady that tested the gunshot residue test, she doesn't know. Detective Fisher and these other detectives, they don't know. And Nicole Sublet she comes in and says now, "Oh no, I didn't see anyone shooting "

What do we know about the key witness in this case, Mr. Antonio Sublet, the second witness that the Commonwealth called? And he's the only one that has come in here claiming that the defendant did the shooting. He's the only one.

Well what else do we know about him? We know he's a convicted felon. And convicted felons are certainly capable of lying. We know he's in jail when the police talked to him, and he didn't go in and volunteer and talk to them.

We know his own cousin, Nicole Sublet, said he was carrying a gun that night, which he denied to the police, and which he denied to you. We know that shells are found right in the area where Antonio Sublet says he was at. He says he was hiding here over this hill, and we know that shells were found there. We also know that a gunshot hole is found in the rear tailgate of Mr. Henry Crawford's truck, who is driving south on 28th street.

Now he comes in and he claims he saw a large man with jewelry and wants you to believe from the distance that he's at hiding, scared, running from the distance he is at, he wants you to believe he could clearly see jewelry. Every time the gun went off, he could see jewelry.

We also know that Antonio later said, "I didn't clearly see the face of the shooter. He says, "I was damn near a block away and I can't clearly say I saw him " Now what should we believe? First the facts are clear that Antonio could have been or was in fact mistaken. He says T *(referring to the defendant)* was wearing a gray t-shirt and jogging pants.

But Nicole says T is wearing white t-shirt and jeans It stands to reason that if he could be mistaken about the clothes, he could just as well be mistaken about who he says was shooting, or what he saw, or if he could see.

I want you to closely look at some of the pictures that the Commonwealth introduced to you. When you get back to he jury room, I want you to look at that bullet hole at the back of Mr. Henry Crawford's truck, who traveling south on 28th street.

Then I want you to look out there at the scene, the morning when all the police got there. It's pretty dark, it's pretty dark now. There are obviously police lights there, and they weren't out there when the shooting happened.

Then I want you to look at this picture. This picture might even give you a little more illumination, because this picture is kind of taken across the street. This is a club. It would appear that this picture is taken right over in this area somewhere. Somebody is standing in the doorway, maybe its two people, maybe its one. It looks like a child. Can you really see who is there?

And if you can't see who is there from that distance, can you really make a quantum leap and try to believe you can see from this distance? Can't see from here, but can see from here. [*Hagan pointing to charts*] Just take these photos back with you and examine them carefully. And then look at this, pretty dark out there, pretty dark.

Of course, one of the witnesses wants us to believe that there is a light in front of the club. You heard Ms. Murphy testify, there is no light out there and she lived there about four years, there is no light.

Antonio said he was even further away, he was over the hill. And that picture is taken right over the street from the club. Could Antonio have been mistaken as to who he saw or what he saw?

And finally, if you think that it is even possible that Antonio could have been mistaken as to whom he saw shooting, then I believe you must find the defendant not guilty, and why do I say that? More than one person is outside the door and more than one person is wearing jewelry. The defendant was at the door pushing people inside or preventing people from getting outside. Antonio probably saw what Nicole saw, the defendant was just pointing and standing at the door, trying to get everybody else to stay inside, so nobody else would be a tragedy on May 17.

And Nicole says Thomas was pointing while he was standing at the door. So it is very likely that if Antonio did see Thomas at the door at some point, he saw Thomas pointing, and mistakenly thought he was shooting.

He first says he didn't see Stephan Rudolph fall. Then he says he did see him fall, kind of inconsistent, kind of changing back and forth. How could he see him fall? If this truck is out there in the street, and you heard the testimony of the detective as to how Mr. Rudolph fell right in front of the truck, I guess he could see through the truck, over the hill, falling down, taking cover, on the ground.

What else should we believe? I believe Antonio Sublett came and lied to you in this courtroom. He wants you to believe that he is the only one at the party not drinking. First he says everyone was drinking at the party, and then when I asked him, "well were you drinking"? "Oh no, I was just kind of laid back." Then he wants you to believe that with all the alcohol around and everyone half drunk, he says people were just drunk and everybody was having a good time, but he is the only sober person is the building.

And he said he didn't have a gun, and that is critical and crucial, because you heard from Tim Howard, who came in here and identified Antonio Sublett as the person that, when a balloon busted, he pulled out the gun and brandished it and said, "I ain't barring none of you niggers in here."

You also heard from Nicole that said the gun fell or dropped out of either his waistband or his pocket. Now why would Antonio come in here and lie about these facts?

Well he's a felon, and convicted felons are certainly not supposed to carry weapons, or use alcohol, or be around alcohol, and if they do, they can have their probation revoked. So if Antonio Sublett admits he did any of these things, he is going to get his probation revoked, and he is going back to jail or the penitentiary.

Finally Antonio has a motive to lie and be dishonest. His friend was shot, his friend died, and he didn't know who did it. So once the police came to him, and showed him some names, and showed him some photographs, of course he is going to put the blame on the defendant.

Of course, if he was at the party that long, he should have known what the defendant was wearing. Blaming the defendant also serves another purpose for Antonio Sublett. It shifts the focus of the investigation from Antonio and his activities that night, and it shifts the focus from little Jo, who Nicole says had a gun and fired it first. And it shifts the focus from Stephan Rudolph, who Jameica says had a gun in the party.

John Balliet questioned one of my last witnesses, Michael Cooper, and he asked Michael Cooper about his name not being on the list. Now the police said when they got there, they said there were eight people on the list.

Jameica Powell wasn't on there. She certainly was there. She gave the party, but her name was not on the list. Lynn Bobbitt, they told you was there, her name was not on the list. George Miller was there and his name is not on the list. Robert Pendleton, the uncle of Michael and Dante Cooper, name is not on the list. Nicole Blake's name is not on the list. We don't know who she is, where she lives, and what she looks like. Michael Stroud he was there, but his name is not on the police list. Kevin Powell he was there, and his name is not on the list.

And then Nicole Sublet came in. She also says, "She didn't see the body drop" but to her recollection, to her recollection, "there was no traffic in the street." Remember that, no traffic in the street. But we've got a body that drops, right in front of the truck, and the guy in the truck gets out and cradles the guy who ends up dead. But she says, "No traffic out there on the street."

Now if she was looking, don't you think she would have saw that truck if she says she saw him fall? Nicole and her cousin obviously got together in the days and weeks and months later, and concocted this story about who shot Stephan Rudolph. They were both friends with Stephan Rudolph.

And no, I'll say it again and again. Stephan Rudolph did not deserve to die like this. Whether he kicked over a table in the club, whether he was drunk, whether he was busting balloons, he did not deserve to die this tragic death. A precious human life was taken, but the problem is that the Commonwealth has not proven this case to you beyond a reasonable doubt.

And then we told you, we promised you at the beginning, that there would be evidence. I told you there would be evidence in this case, evidence of sloppy and poor police work, and I believe that is what you have here.

Will Rogers said it best *"Even if you are on the right track, if you just sit there you will get run over"* and the police certainly sat on this case.

Crucial witnesses are not interviewed, or talked to, or recorded or written statements taken from them in the first 48 hours that the detective said is most critical to solving a homicide case. They did an incomplete investigation. They did no testing of the projectile that came from Mr. Rudolph's body. They had it for nine months, and they could have tested it. We don't know which caliber killed him. We don't know if it was a 32. We don't know if it was a 25. We don't know if it was a 9mm. We don't know if it was a 38.

And all of these people that you have heard testifying that there were a lot of shots being fired. Ms. Murphy says, ten. Then she says twelve to fifteen. It is obviously very dark out there. If that many gun shots are going off, and the police only find four shells? Only four shells? And people were clear in how many shots they heard.

No reconstruction of the homicide scene so you could place Mr. Stephan Rudolph's body. He is lying this way when we got there, head facing this way, legs facing this way, but no reconstruction by them of where the bullets were.

We prepared and brought this chart so you would have a better feel for this case. It's not my job, and it's not your job, and it's not the judge's job to solve a homicide case. It's the police department's job to solve the case, and it is the Commonwealth Attorney's job to prove the defendant guilty beyond a reasonable doubt, and that is what I believe they have failed to do in this case.

No measurements, no measurements of any kind. Not one measurement. Not one person came in here and said they took a measurement of where they found [*Hagan referring to bullets*] these.

Now they said they did measure from the pole, but they didn't take any measurement as to where people were standing, as to where the truck was exactly. I mean, would you guess the truck was approximately here? But the truck could have been here closer to here, but no measurements.

An incomplete and not a thorough investigation in this case. No interviews with many of the witnesses that were still on the scene. Residue tests. It's important to get residue tests, because the lady says, you might be able to tell if a person recently fired or handled, or was near a weapon when it was fired. But her last sentence on that report said "It is inconclusive, this does not mean that the person did not handle or discharge a firearm."

But the important thing is they didn't send the test to the lab until Feb 2nd or 4th. The lab doesn't get it until the 23$^{rd.}$ They don't do the report until the 24th. So if you got a murder trial coming up on the seventeenth of March, you don't have any time to go back and check those witnesses and maybe say, "Well are you sure he didn't have a gun" or try and match up the testimony. Again that's the police's job, and that's the Commonwealth Attorney's job.

EMS, the EMS personnel. I don't believe they were called in, but they could have told us which way they found Mr. Rudolph's body lying. We don't know. We know that one gunshot hit him. There is no controversy about that. I haven't tried to make light of that. No controversy about that. We know it hit him in the lower right portion. We don't know if he was facing south. We don't know if he was facing north, back towards where the truck was, and where Antonio Sublett was, and the way that Nicole Sublett was running, and the way that Little Jo, who fired in the air first, was running. We don't know if he was facing East or West, we just don't know. Again that's not my job, that's not the defendant's job. That's the police's job and that's the Commonwealth Attorney's job.

Now these Instructions you've been given by the judge and you will have a copy back there with you, they say in instruction No. 6. [*Hagan reading instruction on reasonable doubt*] the law presumes a defendant to be innocent. And I pointed that out to you when we were doing jury selection, that the indictment is not evidence or has any weight against him.

But the next sentence says you shall. It didn't say can or maybe. Shall is mandatory. You shall find the defendant not guilty, unless you are satisfied from the evidence alone, and beyond a reasonable doubt that he is guilty.

Not from well it couldn't have happened any other way. That's not from the evidence alone. Well he possibly did it. That's not from the evidence alone and that's not beyond a reasonable doubt. Well he was mad because they disrupted his party, so he must have shot him. That's not from the evidence alone, and that's not beyond a reasonable doubt.

And it also says in the next sentence, [*Hagan reading*] If upon the whole case you have a reasonable doubt that he is guilty, you shall, again mandatory, you don't have an option there, mandatory. If you look at this whole case, and upon this whole case, step back and look at it all, if you have a reasonable doubt, these Instructions, this law, says you must find him not guilty.

Now I can't define reasonable doubt for you. We are not permitted to do that. But I can point out to you some areas, from the evidence alone, from which you might conclude there is reasonable doubt. And if you have these doubts, when you go back to the jury room, point these doubts out to your fellow jurors, whether the doubt comes from a question that I asked, from something a witness said, or from a piece of evidence that's in.

Point out these doubts. Share your doubts about this case with your fellow jurors. And I would submit to you ladies and gentlemen that just one, one single solitary reasonable doubt is sufficient in this case for you to return a verdict of not guilty on all counts, on all of these.

They say we charged him with intentional murder [*Hagan inferring that the charges have now changed*] but now its wanton murder, or its manslaughter 2nd degree, or reckless homicide. To convict this defendant of these charges, you have got to believe and totally believe the testimony of one witness, and that is Antonio Sublett.

DOUBT#1

A number of people were shooting that's obvious. A number of shots were fired. A number of shots were heard. Ms. Murphy said, "I sleep light, but it woke me up. The first shot I heard was boom, boom. It sounded like a loud gun and then I heard a woman scream."

Well you heard Nicole say who fired first, Jo Bartlett. But she wants us to believe he fired in the air. They didn't bring Joe Bartlett in to see which way he shot. Couldn't it have been Jo Bartlett that killed Stephan Rudolph? Couldn't it have been his shot?

Is it possible that when Leola Murphy says she heard the first shot, boom, boom, and a girl screaming, that one of these girls that was near Stephan was screaming, because he was hit with the first shot?

DOUBT #2

Shell casings from three different calibers of weapons 25, 32, 9 mm. Everyone testified that ten to fifteen shots were fired. Where are the other shell casings? Where are they? From this we don't know how many people were shooting. Just because the police found four that doesn't mean they found them all.

So Antonio had a gun he could have been shooting. Little Jo had a gun, and he was shooting, and shells are found in the area where he's standing

DOUBT #3

Jo Bartlett was shooting. What's the use of shooting in the air, if somebody's shooting at you? Why are you going to shoot in the air?

DOUBT #4

Which projectile killed Mr. Rudolph, one of those found, or another one? Which projectile killed Mr. Rudolph? If you are unsure which from which gun came the bullet that killed Stephan Rudolph, then you have a reasonable doubt.

If you are unsure as to which projectile, if you are unsure from which direction the bullet was fired came, then you have a reasonable doubt. If you are unsure about which direction Stephan Rudolph was facing when the shot hit him, then you have a reasonable doubt. Whether the police did a thorough investigation to determine who actually shot Mr. Rudolph, I think that's been clearly shown. They did not.

Ladies and gentlemen you cannot, you cannot render a verdict on this type of evidence. If you do, no one is safe.

DOUBT #5

Residue tests sent to the lab February 4th 1998, nine months after he is killed. They said it doesn't matter when you send them. The results are going to be the same. But you know if you send them in time, you might be able to go back and talk to those witnesses and find out a little more, learn a little more.

I am not going to call it suspicion, I am not going to call it a police cover-up, I am going to call it reasonable doubt.

DOUBT #6

They didn't search John Beamus' house for weapons. They said they searched the way he went, but I don't think the detective could even say which detective searched that way.

DOUBT #7

They didn't find any weapons at the premises. I don't believe any witness testified that they even searched the Lions club to see if anybody in there had weapons. And they didn't take a residue test off of the defendant. They didn't take one off of anybody, but Nathaniel Hickman, Jo Bartlett, and John Beamus. And who did they say they went out of the club with, all of them. Who did they say they left with? Nicole left with Antonio and with Stephan Rudolph.

DOUBT #8

Who put the bullet hole in Mr. Crawford's truck as he's traveling South? They want you to believe that that bullet hole there in the back is going to come from the other direction.

DOUBT #9

If you can reasonably believe that Antonio Sublett made a mistake about the identity of the shooter, then you have a reasonable doubt.

If you are unsure about what distance that Antonio Sublett was, then you probably have a reasonable doubt about his ability to perceive, to accurately perceive who is shooting, particularly when you look at these pictures, particularly when you look at these pictures.

DOUBT #10

If Antonio Sublett comes in here, and he's lying about drinking, he's lying about having a gun and he's unsure, first time "it's a half a block" and he told the police, "I was damn near a block away." He's unsure about his location. Could he also be lying or mistaken about who was doing the shooting, and what he could see?

Finally, as I have indicated ladies and gentlemen it does not become the Court's job, my job, or your job to solve a homicide case. That's the job of the Louisville Division of Police, and that is the job of the Commonwealth of Kentucky to prove this defendant guilty beyond a reasonable doubt. That job always has and always will belong to the Commonwealth.

One last thing that I would ask of you, when I sit down, I won't have a chance to get back up. So don't be in a hurry in this case. Why do I say that? Because the decision that you make will follow this man for the rest of his life. I know that a life was taken, and that is tragic. But the question is, as he said in his opening, the focus is on, have they proven it to you by the evidence. Don't put yourself in the position of having to wrestle with this later, and question whether you did the right thing. Sometimes when you take a stand and stand on principle, you have to stand alone. And if that be the case, so be it.

Stand until hell freezes over. Go back there and do what is right and do not compromise with what is wrong. And I believe that you will conclude as I have that the Commonwealth has not proven this case beyond a reasonable doubt. And yes there is evidence in this case, as I told you from the beginning, evidence that demands a verdict of not guilty. Thank you.

CASE #8

Date of verdict:	October 12, 1999
Charges:	Rape First Degree Class A Felony Sodomy First Degree Class B Felony Robbery First Degree Class B Felony
Possible sentences:	20 to 50 years or Life 10 to 20 years 10 to 20 years
Judge:	Hon. Thomas Knopf, Jefferson Circuit Court
Prosecutor:	Hon. Chad Elder
Defendant's opening argument:	6 ½ minutes
Commonwealth's closing argument:	29 minutes
Defendant's closing argument:	26 minutes
Reasonable Doubt used	20 times
Length of jury deliberations:	3 hours
Was defendant a convicted felon?	NO
Did defendant testify?	YES
VERDICT:	NOT GUILTY on Robbery HUNG JURY on Rape HUNG JURY on Sodomy*

*The Commonwealth elected not to retry the defendant. He entered a plea of guilty to 2 counts of sexual misconduct and was given credit for time served and served an additional 60 days.

SYNOPSIS

On January 4, 1998 the defendant picked up a female late at night. She had been fighting with a girlfriend at a local gay bar named Connections. She claimed he forced her into the car, drove her to some deserted railroad tracks, raped her, forced her to commit oral sodomy, and robbed her of her jewelry.

The defendant testified the sex was consensual and she was given drugs. The rape kit on the victim proved negative and was not put into evidence. The doctor, psychiatrist and rape counselor did not testify. A stipulation was entered into before trial and the defendant admitted that the sperm found on her matched his DNA evidence

The defendant was found **NOT GUILTY** of Robbery 1st and a **HUNG JURY** was declared on the Rape and Sodomy charges, which were later dismissed. The defendant was released after serving nine months in jail.

OPENING STATEMENT

Judge Knopf, Detective McCarthy, Chad Elder, ladies and gentlemen of the jury. Yes, ladies and gentlemen of the jury, I will agree with Chad Elder 100%, rape is a heinous and horrible crime. Women do not ask for, cause, invite, or deserve to be raped.

And I will admit to you several other things. The defendant had sex with the victim on January 4, 1998. And yes his DNA profile matched the sample taken from the victim. And yes the sperm found in the victim came from and belonged to the defendant. But the evidence will be that this was not sex by forcible compulsion. This was consensual sex between two consenting adults. And the evidence will be that, no, he did not take her jewelry, her money, her cigarette lighter, or ten dollars from her. And the police went over to his house and searched his house sometime later, and they took jewelry, but it wasn't her jewelry. They took earrings. She didn't even say an earring was missing. The clothes they found were not the clothes she said he was wearing.

There will not be one shred of evidence, other than what the victim says, that this was anything other than consensual sex. Now she was taken to the University of Louisville Hospital, immediately after she was in the car with Detective Bailey, or after she had been talking with Detective McCarthy, and the hospital did a physical exam on her, they did a genital exam on her, and they did what is required by law, which is a rape kit.

And what did the hospital find? No lacerations. No cuts. No scars. No trauma to the genital area or the rest of her body. No bruises, no fractures, or none of that. They found nothing, because all this was was consensual sex between two consenting adults. The hospital did find some wounds on her, however these were wounds that she said she self-inflicted. She tried to commit suicide. The victim and her girlfriend Missy were at Connections, a local gay bar. And they got into a fight when she saw Missy talking to another girl. And after that fight. They were both thrown out of the club, and she's walking home. Well she's obviously upset. She's crying. Her weekend that she was supposed to spend with Missy has been turned all upside down. She's walking home.

The defendant borrows a car. He's in another part of town and he borrows a car from a guy by the name of Mike. And he is in that car and he is riding. He's dropped off a buddy of his and they get some cigarettes and alcohol. He gets to the corner of 1st and Breckinridge, and it's at 1st and Breckinridge that there is a phone booth on the northeast corner, The defendant is using or attempting to use that phone. He sees a young lady over across the street. He goes over and strikes up a conversation with the young lady and asks her, "What are you doing walking in this area at this time of night"? This is over near the Old SanAntonio Inn (*high crime area*). She explains that she's upset and she's crying. Her and this girlfriend have had a fight, and she's tried to commit suicide. There are fresh marks on hers arms and on both hands. And the defendant says, "I'll give you a ride or you can come and ride with me." She agrees to get in the car and it's only her and the defendant. She gets in the car and they ride around 4th street in Old Louisville. And they are over near 6th & Shipp, and of course the defendant says "I'd like to have sex with you, and in exchange for that sex with you, I'll give you some drugs." She says show me what you've got. He shows her a small amount of drugs. They agreed to have sex. They go back near the railroad tracks. Its maybe 1, 2 or 3 o'clock in the morning and its about 57 degrees so its not really cold as it usually is in January. They go back there and do whatever they agreed to do together. I don't have to go into all those details because they agreed to do it. As the defendant is getting ready to get up, now she has taken all of her clothes off, but the defendant has only pulled his pants down. He pulls his pants up and he says, "I'm out of here." She says, "Where are you going"? "I've got to go home, my girlfriend is waiting on me." The defendant gets ready to leave, and she says don't leave me wait on me. She leaves her panties and her bra there and pulls the rest of her clothes on, and gets back in the car, gets back in the car with the defendant for him to drop her off.

   Now we are here today, and the evidence will show we are here today, for whatever reason the victim decides when she sees a police car. She decides to flag a police car down and says she has been raped, and the evidence will show that she did flag that police car down. The defendant goes on home and drops his car off, abandons his car and he goes on home.

   We don't know why the lady says she was raped. I don't think we will find that out from the evidence, but the evidence will be that she flags a police car down and says she has been raped. Maybe because she's upset, maybe because she has had unprotected sex, and maybe she's trying to get back at her friend Missy. All the defendant knows is this was consensual sex. Maybe if he had dropped her off at home, maybe we wouldn't be here today. We don't know that. But you will see and the evidence will be that there are no signs of rough sex, or anything but consensual sex.

Your job in this case is to be fair to do the right thing, to do the right thing in this case. I ask that you listen to all of the evidence, and don't form an opinion until you have heard all of the evidence. I am convinced you will return a verdict of not guilty as to this defendant on all of these charges. Thank You.

CLOSING ARGUMENT

May it please the Court, Honorable Judge Knopf, Mr. Dilger, Officer Heady, Mr. Mullins, the defendant, ladies and gentlemen of the jury. First of all and once again let me say thanks on behalf of myself, as an officer of the Court, and on behalf of the defendant. Jurors don't often get appreciated enough for the valuable service they provide. You provide a valuable service.

It is very important that you listen to what I say because this is not a game of cat and mouse. I don't get to get up again. This is my only chance to say something to you on behalf of the defendant. Under our system the prosecution gets the last word so it's important that you listen at this time to what I say on his behalf and how I am summarizing the evidence.

Our job is over. My job as defense counsel, Chad's job as prosecutor for the Commonwealth, Detective McCarthy's job, the judge job as judge and referee. Our job is over and yours is about to begin. You have a solemn task to which you have sworn an oath. You said that when we selected you that you would do the right thing, you would be fair in this case.

And ladies and gentlemen, I would submit to you that there is evidence in this case. There is evidence. Missing evidence, valuable information, maybe an incomplete police investigation. But there is evidence in this case, evidence that demands a verdict of not guilty.

At the beginning of this case and when we selected you as jurors, we asked you whether you understood that because this is a criminal case and because they were trying to send this young man to the penitentiary for twenty years, we asked you whether you understood that the law accorded him some protections. And you said you understood that. And we went over those protections and some of those protections are in these Instructions the Judge has given you.

That the indictment is not evidence, and has no weight against him, and that the burden of proof is on the Commonwealth in this case. That burden never shifts to the defendant. That burden always stays on the Commonwealth. And we don't have to prove or disprove their story. That's their burden. They have to carry that burden.

And we asked you whether you understood that the defendant comes into this courtroom with the presumption of innocence, and that presumption stays with him throughout this trial and until you return a verdict.

We also asked you whether you understood that you can't

decide this case on sympathy or emotion, sympathy for Ms. Thompson or sympathy for the defendant. You have got to decide this case on the evidence that comes from that chair, and the Instructions of law as given to you by the Court.

And you also said that you understood that you would be following the law if you looked Mr. Elder in the eye and said to him as Commonwealth's Attorney, you did not meet your burden, you did not prove your case beyond a reasonable doubt. And you are still following the law when you do that.

And finally you said that you understood that the standard by which we judge this case is the standard as the judge has given you, proof beyond a reasonable doubt, as to each and every element of each one of these three offenses. It is proof beyond a reasonable doubt. And we said it wasn't enough for the Commonwealth to show that he is possible guilty, probably guilty, or there is a strong suspicion of guilt. But they have got to prove him guilty beyond a reasonable doubt.

And on Instruction No. 4, if you want to turn to that it would be okay. And the Judge has basically given it to you the way I said it.*[Hagan reading the Instruction word for word]* The law presumes a defendant to be innocent of a crime and the indictment shall not be considered as having any weight against him. Shall is a mandatory word. It does not say may, it says shall. *[continues reading]* You shall find the defendant not guilty, unless you are satisfied from the evidence alone, not from anything else, but from the evidence alone, and beyond a reasonable doubt that he is guilty.

Then it says if upon the whole case you have a reasonable doubt that he is guilty, you shall find him not guilty. Just stand back, and look at this whole case and say there is some doubt in my mind. If upon the whole case you have a reasonable doubt, its mandatory, it says you shall find him not guilty.

Now during my opening I believe we promised you several things. We promised you we would show you that the defendant did have sex with Ms. Thompson. And he admitted that, consensual sex with her. That his DNA profile matched and that was his sperm that they found on Ms. Thompson. But we also said that, other than the testimony of the victim, there wouldn't be one shred of evidence that this was anything other than consensual sex. No weapons. No torn clothing. No lacerations. No bruises. No blood. No tears to her vagin, as she says the hospital told her.

But the Commonwealth also made you some promises, and I took notes during their opening as I usually do. The Commonwealth said we are going to give you the evidence, and you decide what happened. Well I am convinced that they did not give you all the evidence.

Where is the doctor that examined Ms. Thompson? Where is the psychiatrist that examined Ms. Thompson? Where is the rape counselor that examined Ms. Thompson or talked to Ms. Thompson? None of those people were here to testify. Once again, it's not our burden, it's their burden. And they said that a rape kit was performed. I asked Detective McCarthy, "Do you have the rape kit"? No. The doctor is not here, the rape kit is not here. Once again, it's their burden.

Ladies and gentlemen we are talking about the Commonwealth Attorneys office. They can get any witness, they can get the Commonwealth's detectives to go out and drag a witness in here if they won't come in here voluntarily. They've got the entire Louisville Police Department at their disposal to talk to witnesses and to get witnesses in here. They've got the Kentucky State Crime lab at their disposal. But for some reason we don't bring in the doctors, we don't bring in the psychiatrist, we don't bring in the rape counselor, on a case where they want to send him to the penitentiary for twenty years.

And finally they said, "we want you to hold the defendant accountable for what he stole from her that night, a sense of security, as he dumped her on Fourth Street." Now I am wondering whether that word dumped her on Fourth Street, did that come from Ms. Thompson, or did that come from the Commonwealth.

And maybe that's the reason why we are here. And maybe he should have taken her home. But he didn't take her home. And maybe that's the only reason she went to the police and said she had been raped, because he didn't give her a ride home.

It is obvious to me, and I think it might be obvious to some of you, that the Commonwealth has defaulted on the promises made to you. Instead of keeping or honoring their promises, this case has come back marked insufficient evidence.

You know they did DNA on him, and we got hung up or there was some confusion about whether he read the report or when the DNA came back. That's not an issue, because we admitted that from the opening. We admitted that it was his DNA. So why go into all of that. That's to divert you from the main issues in this case.

Why do a rape kit on the victim and a rape kit on him. You get his evidence in here, and you don't bring her evidence in here. Now is that fair? If it can happen to him, it can happen to any of us. Remember once, again it's their burden. It is not our burden. We don't have to do anything.

Now these Instructions, on page 6 under definitions, if you will turn to that Instruction. Let's first go to Instruction number 3. I'm sorry, let's go to number 1.One and two because 1 & 2 have the same under b. *[reading from the Instructions]* Only if you believe from the evidence beyond a reasonable doubt that in this county he engaged in sexual intercourse. Well you shouldn't have any problem deciding that because we admitted that. Same thing to sodomy, he engaged in deviate sexual intercourse. He agreed that they had oral sex. But it comes down to part #2, that he did so by forcible compulsion. And then when you turn back to the definitions #4, what does forcible compulsion say?

Forcible compulsion means physical force or threat of physical force, express or implied, which places a person in ear of immediate death immediate death or physical injury... Have you heard any evidence from that witness chair that Ms. Thompson was placed in fear of immediate death or physical injury? Where is the proof? I would submit to you that it is totally lacking in this case.

And then when you get to the Instruction #3 on the robbery. That he stole property from her, which of course is in dispute. He says he took nothing from her. She says he took her jewelry lighter and cigarettes, some confusion about the lighter and cigarettes, some confusion. Police officer says, "Well I got a pager and a lighter. And I remember because the pager kept going off." She wants you to believe he took everything, that there was a bracelet on her arm. The detective said, his report said "bracelets" it didn't say one bracelet, with one s.

But it says "and that in the course of doing," in the course of doing what? That means that in the course of committing, stealing the property from her, and with the intent to accomplish the theft, he used physical force. Now what evidence was there that he used physical force, in the course of committing that theft? When? Now, not back when she got in the car and the way she said she got in, but in the course of committing that theft, and stealing that property from her. I would submit to you there is no evidence of force that came from that witness chair.

Ladies and gentlemen you are asked and called upon to ask to do a job that the Commonwealth should have done. They didn't and now you are called upon to decide. Yes, we will give you the evidence and let you decide what happened.

I say in this case; no evidence of force, no evidence of immediate death, no evidence of physical injury, no evidence in the course of committing the theft-- no rape, no robbery, and no sodomy.

No weapons were ever found or described--again, no rape, no robbery, and no sodomy. I didn't ask the question, Chad Elder asked the question. "When he pulled you, were you scared. No. You can remember the testimony.

And then these medical records; these medical records say this happened in Louisville in a deserted house. But you heard her say it happened out in the woods. No restraints were used on her. No foreign objects were used on her. Physical examination-negative. and you will get these records to take back there with you.

All blanks, all blanks except arms, self inflicted wounds prior to the assault, and then this other sheet, "she says she was abducted from near the car wash at First and Jacob." This says abducted from front of house.

Now ladies and gentlemen, too many inconsistencies, too many contradictions, too many things that don't add up in this case, that should give you a reasonable doubt. No restraints used, no force. "I wanted to hurt myself." No trauma, no lacerations, multiple superficial lacerations to both arms and fresh scabs.

Once again, I say no force from the evidence, not from what we think, but from the evidence. They are required to put on the proof. We are not required to put on the proof. And then she says that the hospital told hers she had a tear in her vagina. Don't you think that if the hospital told her they would bring those physicians in here to prove that very fact. That would be the force and that would be the injury.

And then, U of L. She wants to say that the University of Louisville hospital which is the designated hospital in our community where you take victims of sexual assault. "Well they misrepresented me. They misread me or they weren't paying attention to what I was saying."

I don't believe that for a moment, ladies and gentlemen, and I don't think you do either. If there was a sign of force, they would have used every subpoena power that this Commonwealth Attorney's office has to get those doctors in here and to get them to testify. Because the evidence is contrary and goes against everything that Ms. Thompson says happened in this case. And once again we don't have to prove anything.

And we know that she was extremely upset. She just had a fight, but now she comes in and she tells you, "Oh it was not a fight, it was an argument. No, we did not get thrown out." I am sure many of you have been in a bar. You get in a fight and you get thrown out. It was a fight. Three times in the detectives report. It was a fight. It was not an argument. Now who is she trying to fool?

If you have a doubt like I have do in this case, I asked you to share your doubts that you have with your fellow jurors in this case. Whether the doubt comes from something I asked, from something a witness said, or from something you picked up from the testimony. Share your doubts with your fellow jurors.

And I would submit to you ladies and gentlemen that just

one, you don't need a whole lot, just one single solitary reasonable doubt is sufficient in this case for you to return a verdict of not guilty on all counts against the defendant--just one.

And I can't possibly go over all the doubts in this case. You heard the testimony. You can remember what you heard and what you saw from the witness stand. But I thought I ought to at least list some of these and let the Commonwealth explain to you how they resolved these doubts.

Doubt #1 forcible compulsion

Physical force which places a person in fear of immediate death or physical injury. No proof here. No proof, I say no conviction.

Doubt #2 physical injuries to Ms. Thompson

And no the victim doesn't have to resist in a rape. We all know that is what the law says. And I told you that rape is a horrible heinous and vile crime, and no woman deserves to be raped. No person deserves to be sexually assaulted. But where is the proof in this case? So many inconsistencies, so many things unanswered. The police didn't go back and ask her a second time, or interview here to try and to clear up some of these inconsistencies.

They interviewed her one time. One time and that was it, on a rape case that they want to use to send him to the penitentiary for twenty years. One time, not to clear up where she was abducted from, not to clear up where this happened "in a deserted house," not to clear up descriptions of him. What is she trying to do? She is trying to throw the police off. She is extremely upset. She can't go with her girlfriend that weekend. What is she trying to do, and who is she trying to fool? And then she is traumatically raped and sodomized and robbed. But she doesn't go for any follow up treatment.

And you heard no evidence and saw no proof, anything about what happened to here afterwards; days afterwards, weeks afterwards, and months afterwards. I understand it is now a year and seven or eight months later, but you didn't hear any proof as to how she was feeling in February or March of 1998.

Wouldn't you think that would be important for a person that would be the victim of a rape, sodomy, and robbery? She might have nightmares. She might be hallucinating. She might be scared to walk down the street, but you didn't hear any proof cause there was no proof.

And then DOUBT #4 as to where she is picked up from

You know that might have started the police on the right path to really solving what was happening, or what was going on out there. If she is inconsistent on that, she is inconsistent on the rest of it. From

First and Jacob, to in front of my apartment, it doesn't match up.

The question was asked. I don't know if I asked it or they asked it. Whether she was threatened in the car? No. Did she feel unsafe as she was riding? No.

And then we get into who he gave the car to afterwards. Ladies and gentlemen what does that have to do with a rape robbery and sodomy, who he gave the car to? What does that have to do with it, whether he told the police something that wasn't true or not? He's not on trial here for stealing a car. He's on trial for rape robbery and sodomy.

And then they tried to make light of the fact that he refused to sign this waiver of rights form. Let me read that to you ladies and gentlemen because that's important. [*reading rights waiver form*] It's important for him and it's important for all of us.

YOUR RIGHTS

1. Before we ask you questions, you must understand your rights.
2. You have the right to remain silent
3. Anything you say can and will be used against you in a court of law.
4. You have the right to talk to a lawyer prior to any questioning or the making of any statements, and to have him present with you while you are being questioned.
5. If you cannot afford to hire a lawyer, one will be appointed by the Court to represent you before any questioning, if you desire one.
6. You may stop the questioning or the making of a statement at any time, or by refusing to answer further, or by requesting to consult with an attorney prior to continuing with the questioning or the making of any statements.

That's your rights and that's my rights. But of course they want to make light of the fact that he refused to sign this. Says you can stop them at any time, and don't have to say one thing further. Don't have to give your name any further. Don't have to say anything. You can just remain mute. But what does that have to do with whether he raped, sodomized, or robbed Ms. Thompson on January 4, 1998? I would say nothing.

Finally ladies and gentlemen, don't be in a hurry on this case. The decision that you make today, the decision that each one of you twelve make, that decision that you make will follow the defendant for the rest of his life. And don't put yourself in a position of having to wrestle with this later on to determine whether I made the right decision, or whether I was hurried in my decision. You might feel he shouldn't have propositioned her. You might have feel he shouldn't have picked up a total stranger out on the street. You might feel like he shouldn't have had unprotected sex with her. Ladies and gentlemen, he's not on trial for any of that. He's on trial for rape robbery and sodomy. You might feel he shouldn't have had drugs on him or offered her drugs for sex. That's well and good, but once again he's not on trial for that. As I indicated to you in the opening rape is a violent and horrible crime, and no woman, man, or child deserves to be sexually assaulted.

When you go back to that jury room, I am going to ask you to stand. Stand. Sometimes when you stand on principle you might have to stand alone. But when you go back to that jury room, stand. And if you have to, stand until hell freezes over. Go back there and do the right thing in this case, and don't be compromised into doing what you feel is wrong. Thank you ladies and gentlemen.

CASE #9

Date of verdict:	August 31, 2000
Charges:	Trafficking in Controlled Substance First Degree Class C Felony
	Trafficking in Controlled Substance Third Degree Class A Misd.
	Persistent Felony Offender
	Failure to be in Possession of Operators License
Possible sentences:	5 to 10 years
	12 months in jail and/or $500 fine
	10 to 20 years
	90 days in jail and/or $250.00 fine
Judge:	Hon. Geoffrey Morris, Jefferson Circuit Court
Prosecutor:	Hon. Craig Dilger
Defendant's opening argument:	4 minutes
Defendant's closing argument:	31 minutes
Commonwealth's closing argument:	20 minutes
Reasonable Doubt used	27 times
Length of jury deliberations:	60 minutes
Was defendant a convicted felon?	YES
Did defendant testify?	NO
Verdict:	**NOT GUILTY**

SYNOPSIS

The defendant, a bricklayer, and a co-worker were both charged with Trafficking in Cocaine and Trafficking in Diazepam and Complicity. The defendant, a convicted felon, was also charged with being a Persistent Felony Offender II, and No Operator's License.

On March 17, 2000 undercover veteran narcotics officers say they saw the defendant's vehicle back into a driveway, and engage in what appeared to be a drug transaction. He pulled in, had a conversation with someone that came out of the house, and pulled off. The defendant says he had just left work, and was on his way to the bank to get money to pay the crew that worked for him

The officers decided to pull him over and asked everyone to exit the vehicle. The defendant was searched and found to have $843 in small bills and a cell phone. His two passengers were also searched. The second defendant had eight individually wrapped pieces of crack cocaine that dropped from his pocket or waistband and in plain view. The cocaine had a street value of $250. A third passenger, who was in the back seat, and a possible informant were let go.

The trial lasted a day and a half with neither the 1st or 2nd defendant taking the stand. The 2nd defendant, through his lawyer, admitted that the cocaine was his, and that he had it for his own personal use. The jury deliberated 60 minutes and found the 1st defendant **NOT GUILTY** of all charges, except no operators license (later dismissed as valid by the Court).

The second defendant represented by the Hon. Paul J. Mullins was found **NOT GUILTY** of Trafficking in Cocaine and **NOT GUILTY** of Trafficking in Diazepam, but **GUILTY** of Possession of Cocaine, Schedule I (which he admitted during trial).

OPENING STATEMENT

Honorable Judge Morris, Mr. Dilger, Officer Heady, both defendants, Mr. Mullins, ladies and gentlemen of the jury. This case might be simple, but it's very serious and very important because police officers and Commonwealth Attorneys have a lot of power. They have the power to decide who gets charged and who doesn't.

And maybe that's the reason that Mr. Dilger told you about the 3rd person in the car, because today, as we stand here, they wouldn't give us the name of the person who was in the car, they wouldn't give us the name of the person who was in the house. [Objection by the Commonwealth-Overruled by the Court]. You will not here one officer come in here today and say that he saw my client in possession of either diazepam or cocaine. He was in possession of a phone and $843.00.

Now the fact that I have a phone today and some money in my pocket [*Hagan pulling out his cell phone and some money and waving to jury*] doesn't make me a drug dealer. Now they want you to make a quantum leap.

You will see from the evidence. [*pointing to defendant #1*] He is in the driver's seat and he's driving. [*pointing to defendant #2*] He's in the passenger seat. There is someone else in the seat behind him. There is another individual that comes out of the house.

Now this is at 10:30 at night, and we've got some pictures of the house, which they now say is under surveillance. But you will learn from the police report which says "they were watching." Now on the day of trial it's under surveillance, but be that as it may "under surveillance or watching it."

And you will see it's almost impractical to see what's going on in a car from that distance at 10:30 at night. It's not an area where there is a lot of light. There are street lights, I'm sure, but it's not a well lit area. So when that evidence comes in you have got to look at it to see if you can see what they saw.

They follow these gentlemen as they come out of the driveway. They pull him over in the 4500 block of Poplar Level Road, right near the Sports Spectrum and the Thornton's gas station. They get all three of them out of the car.

Out of his pocket [*pointing to defendant #2*] falls cocaine. There is a pill bottle on the floorboard of the car. The only thing they got off of this defendant was a cell phone and $843.00. Now why did he have that $843.00?

Now ladies and gentlemen, I will tell you right from the outset, my client is not a saint. Whatever he has done in the past is in the past and he's paid for that. He came out and he's tried to straighten his life up. He went into the bricklaying business. He's a pretty good bricklayer. He's doing houses in Park Duvalle, Wolfpen Branch, and on that particular day, he's doing a house in Stone Ledges in Fern Creek. But a lot of bricklayers get paid in cash. A lot of times the people that work for them want to get paid in cash. It's Friday and he goes and picks up the money.

Sometimes the guys are still on the work site, and sometimes they are gone, and you have to go find them and pay them. That's why he's got the cash. You will not hear one iota of evidence that my client had anything on him other than a cell phone and money. Ladies and gentlemen that's not evidence of trafficking, and that's not evidence of possession.

At the end of this case, I'll be back up here again, and I'll be asking you to hold the Commonwealth's feet to the fire, and make them dot every "I" and cross every "T". And I'll be asking you to return a verdict of not guilty. Thank You.

CLOSING ARGUMENT

May it please the Court, Honorable Judge Morris, Mr. Dilger, Officer Heady, Mr. Mullins, the defendants, ladies and gentlemen of the jury. First of all let me say thank you to each one of you twelve jurors for your time and patience in this case.

We couldn't do our jobs if we didn't have jurors willing to sit in judgment of fellow citizens, and who were willing to come and do as our criminal justice system requires, and base a verdict on evidence and the Instructions of law as given to you by the Court. So I want to say thank you.

Let me put the bottom line right at the top. This case stinks and it stinks to high heaven. You know why it stinks? It stinks because as I indicated to you in voir dire, these people [*pointing to Commonwealth Attorney and lead officer*] have a lot of power. They have the power to charge, the power to not charge, they have the power to decide who gets arrested and who doesn't get arrested. They have the power to decide how to handle the evidence, and how not to handle the evidence

And what makes me angry and mad, even though I have been in this business 21 years, is when people play less than honest, and less than candid, and less than fair; fair with the court, fair with the defendants and their lawyers, and fair with you as jurors.

We are talking about a lot of things in this case that are missing. We are talking about missing material witnesses. The officer didn't want to say that was a material witness, but when I broke it down for him he had to admit, "Yes, those were material witnesses." Where are they?

Missing money? We don't find out until today, the second day of this trial, that the Jefferson County Police Department Metro Narcotics have now instituted a new policy where evidence in a criminal case goes to the property room, and then goes to the bank, literally destroyed. Done away with, not here for you to view, and not available for the defense to test. Gone!

The evidence, that money, did not belong to these officers. It didn't belong to the Jefferson County Police Department. It was his money that came out of his pocket. And if it belonged anywhere, it belonged in this courtroom, brought into you here in an evidence packet, but it's gone.

And at the beginning of this case, I asked you whether you understood certain things and you said that you did. You said you understood that the indictment was not evidence, and that the burden of proof is on the Commonwealth. It started on the Commonwealth it stays on the Commonwealth, and it never shifts to the defendant.

You said you understood that the defendant comes into this Court, and even now he is presumed to be innocent of this crime, and that the burden of proof that is established by our criminal justice system, and Judge Morris told you, it's the highest burden, "proof beyond a reasonable doubt." And you said you understood that you could only decide this case based on two things. You can decide it based on the evidence that came from that witness chair, [*pointing to witness chair*] and you can decide it based on the Instructions of law as given to you by the court.

And these Instructions say... Of course, we come in and he's charged with trafficking in a controlled substance, cocaine 1st degree, schedule II, or trafficking in controlled substance in the 3rd degree schedule IV diazepam. But now you have an either or. We can't hook him on one, so let's get him on the lesser included offense, possession. First it was trafficking, now it is trafficking or possession. They want to make it a guessing game for you as jurors.

And then in this, I'm sorry in Instruction No. 1, [*Hagan reads Instruction No. 1 while holding it aloft for jury who is following along with their copies*], you will find the defendant guilty under this instruction, if and only if you believe from the evidence, and beyond a reasonable doubt all of the following... that in Jefferson County, KY.

No question about where it happened. We know we are in Jefferson County, nobody's disputed that. On or about the 17th date of March..., no dispute about the date, the defendant acting...Now what did they prove about how he was acting? They didn't say one word that he said to Barry Yocum. They didn't give you one transaction. No money to Ted. No drugs to Ted. Not even a glance at Ted, and not even a handshake with Ted.

[*Hagan continues to read*] ...had in his possession cocaine. Did they ever show you from any of the five or six witnesses that they brought in here, that he had in his possession a quantity of cocaine?

Not from that officer, not from this officer, not from the canine officer, not from the lab expert, not from Detective Pope and not from Officer Puckett. It's the same thing as to the diazepam. They didn't show it was in his possession, but these Instructions require you to find beyond a reasonable doubt that he had it in his possession. And I circled it on here, had it in his possession. And then, so if you don't try to get him on trafficking, hook him in on complicity.

[*Hagan reading complicity instruction*] Complicity means that a person is guilty of an offense committed by another person when, with the intention of promoting or facilitating the commission of that offense, he solicits commands or engages in a conspiracy with such other person to commit the offense.

They never showed you any transaction, any conspiracy, any

planning about this offense between my client and him, or my client and anyone else and possession means to have actual physical possession or otherwise exercise dominion or control over tangible physical objects.

What witness showed you that my client had actual physical possession, or exercised any dominion or control over this pill bottle or this cocaine? And we didn't dispute that it was cocaine. He didn't have to drag that lady in here. And we didn't dispute the chain of custody. Why bring him in here? That's an effort to build a case where there is no case.

[*Hagan pointing to reasonable doubt chart on board and reading*] Finally you said that you understood that the proof that is necessary and this is what the judge has instructed you. The law presumes a defendant to be innocent of a crime, and the indictment is not any evidence and can not be considered as evidence or as having any weight against him, and you shall find the defendant not guilty, it says not guilty first, unless you are satisfied from the evidence alone.

Not from what might have happened, not from what must have been going on, not from what the officer thought was going on, not from what perhaps happened, not from what the officer suspected happened, not because the officer believed, in his opinion, the defendant was engaged in a drug transaction.

But from the evidence alone that he is guilty, and if upon the whole case, I going to use the officer's words "totality." If you look at the whole circumstances of what was going on, and you have a doubt, a reasonable doubt of the circumstances, if upon the whole case you have a doubt reasonable doubt that he is guilty, you shall find him not guilty. Just step back from the case. Just take a look at the whole thing. Something is not right, something is not clicking here.

And the defendant is not compelled to testify, and the fact that he did not testify cannot be used or an inference of guilt drawn, and should not prejudice him in any way. The Commonwealth alone has to paint the picture of guilt beyond a reasonable doubt.

And during my opening, I promised you we would show you several things. I promised you that nobody would say my client was in possession of any drugs, or any pill bottles. And that nobody would say that my client gave him any money in exchange for drugs. I promised you what we would show. I ask you to judge whether we kept our promises.

Now I took notes during the Commonwealth's opening and they promised you several things. They promised you they would bring in six or seven witnesses and that they would all be police officers. No civilian witnesses, and why is that? Because they don't know the two material witnesses, even though they id them and checked for warrants.

Now ladies and gentlemen if you don't believe that over there in the Jefferson County police department there is a recorder recording everything that is called in, then I am not standing here.

There are no witnesses regarding the transaction. Nobody can say, this officer, that officer, the two lead officers, nobody can say my client had any drugs, transferred or sold any drugs, manufactured any drugs or dispensed any drugs, or possessed any drugs with intent to sell them.

And then only when it gets to the day of the trial, do were here that there is a short exchange at the side of the Ford Explorer. When the police stopped these two they got a lucky hit. And that happens in police work. He *(co-defendant #2)* had drugs on him, these two. But they didn't get any evidenceon this man *(co-defendant #1)*, and they should not have stopped him, and we should not be in this courtroom today.

It is obvious that the Commonwealth has defaulted on its promises as far as this evidence is concerned. This case is a sham. Instead of honoring and keeping the promise made to you, they have given you a bad check, a check that has come back marked insufficient evidence.

It was the writer, *James Baldwin* that said, "*The moment we break faith with our promises, or with one another, the sea engulfs us and the light goes out.*" And I believe that the light has gone out on the Commonwealth's case as far as the evidence in this case is concerned.

No matter what you think, and I detest people that sell drugs, but I have to defend them, that's my livelihood. What we think about dope dealers and drug dealers or whatever, that's not to be used as evidence.

It is only the evidence that comes from that witness chair. I believe it was *Will Rogers* that said, "*Even if you are on the right track, if you just sit there you will get run over.*" The police certainly sat on this one. They did an incomplete investigation. They did no follow up investigation to find out whose drugs those were, or if there were fingerprints on those drugs. They did not send the money to the lab, money that is now missing, gone, and destroyed. They did not send it to the lab to get it washed for drug residue. Don't know whose name is on the cellular phone. Don't know which house was under surveillance, either by the first group of officers, or the second group of officers.

Confused as to whether or not the car pulled into or backed into the driveway. That is kind of important. Maybe some of you don't think that is important, because maybe if you are backing in the driveway, you have something to hide. One says he pulled in. One says he backed in I don't know which one it is.

Do you think that in a homicide case the Commonwealth would throw away the gun? Don't let it happen in this case. This is just as important as a homicide case.

And my pictures, they might not be perfect pictures. You can take them to the jury room. But I am referring to exhibits 1, 2, 3, and 4. They've got photographers over there. They can certainly go out and take pictures to show you the vantage point from which they were sitting and so they could observe what was going on, lots of bushes and trees out there. They didn't bring in any pictures because they couldn't see what was going on.

They got a lucky hit. They made a bad arrest of my client. They didn't have the guts to realize it and dismiss this case. Nobody is calling these officers liars. I believe every word they said. They didn't write it down, they forgot about it. Evidence is gone. It's not their fault, but it's somebody's fault. You just don't throw away material evidence in a criminal case.

That shouldn't happen in America, in our democracy, and under our system of laws. We are not ruled by the law of the jungle. We are a country of laws. This case didn't deserve to be in this courtroom. You don't send somebody to the penitentiary on this kind of evidence, because if you do, none of us are safe, none of us are safe. If it could happen to him, it could happen to anybody. Lose evidence, can't find the names, don't disclose the witnesses, change the stories when you come to trial.

Ladies and gentlemen suspicion is not proof. I know what they suspected. That's their job, and most of them [*referring to the police*] do a good job.

If you have doubts like I do, when you go back to the jury room, tell your fellow jurors about the doubts that you have about this case. Whether it comes from the evidence, or from something I said, or from something you picked up on. Tell your fellow jurors about the reasonable doubts that you have in this case.

And I submit to you that you don't have to have a hundred doubts, you don't have to have fifty. I submit to you that one single solitary reasonable doubt is sufficient for you to return a verdict of not guilty for the defendant in this case. But I wrote down a couple, I wrote down six.

Doubt #1

Did any witness testify from that chair as to seeing Barry Yocum manufacture, sell, transfer, or possess with the intent to sell any cocaine or diazepam.

Doubt #2

Any proof from the evidence alone that Barry Yocum had in his possession that pill bottle, or ever touched that pill bottle.

Doubt #3

Any proof that came from the evidence alone that Barry's hard earned money had cocaine residue on it. They could have sent it to the KY State Crime lab, could have sent it to the DEA lab, and could have sent it to the FBI crime lab. They chose to do none of the above.

Doubt #4

Any proof from the evidence alone that will show that there was a solicitation, command, engagement in a conspiracy, or an attempt to aid in the planning or committing, with both defendants and anybody else. And Mr. McMurray shocked me when he said sometimes we believe and suspect that its dope, and sometime its not. It's the latter in this case. They didn't witness it. They didn't have the evidence. They didn't have the guts enough to dismiss it, or not to charge my client, or to dismiss these charges.

And then the missing money, at the last hour, with no notice. Its like a bicycle, it won't go up a hill without a chain or pedal.

The guy came in and told you he paid him $2500.00. No doubt about it, the defendant is a bricklayer. Now if he's paid $7500 for one house, he's making pretty good money. After ten houses, he's made $75,000.

It's not all his. He's got to pay his workers a substantial amount of money. Evidently he's doing pretty good houses. Those houses look pretty good. You take the pictures back there and look at them. You heard the gentlemen say he had no problem with his work. The quality of his work was excellent. And these people want to be paid in cash, because a lot of builders go under and run out and people don't get paid. Said he wouldn't dare pay them all the money up front. You would never get the job done.

He's not an angel. None of us are angels. But the question is whether they have proved his guilt beyond a reasonable doubt?

What does the evidence mean in this case. Missing material witnesses, to me it means **reasonable doubt**. Evidence not properly handled or fingerprinted, **reasonable doubt**. Money allegedly hit on by the dog is not later tested for residue. No follow up or follow through, **reasonable doubt**. Pulling in or backing in, **reasonable doubt**. And then the pretext that this was a traffic stop. This wasn't a traffic stop. He had not violated any traffic laws, and the officer can't tell that if you are driving down the road. I know I have forgotten my license on plenty of occasions. But the officer can't tell, sitting in his car, whether you've got your license on you. It's supposed to be on you. I will admit that. How is he going to know that? They are not mind readers.

If it was a traffic stop, it would have been on the citation as to what traffic law he violated. You know speeding too fast, speeding 55 in a 35, or reckless driving, or careless driving. Just put that on there so we can get away with stopping him.

No pictures of the scene. And we don't know who owns or lives in that house. The Jefferson County Police Department has more ample resources so we could tell who lives in that house.

You might say we can tell that. Once again, it is not my job, it is not Mr. Mullins job, and it's none of our jobs. It is the Commonwealth attorney's and the police officers responsibility to prove to you guilt in this case beyond a reasonable doubt.

Don't let them shift this burden to the defendant. That's what they get paid for. That's what our tax dollars pay them to do. Don't let them shift that burden to the defendant. And they are watching the house or on surveillance. To me, surveillance says that you are going to have cameras and you are going to have tape recorders. They didn't have any of that. Just a lucky hit!

Stop the car and the guy just happens to have drugs on him. They won't you to make a quantum leap from possession on one passenger, to trafficking on another passenger. Then a third passenger is let go, and the person at the house is let go. The integrity of the evidence is certainly suspect in this case as to what you can accept for beyond a reasonable doubt.

And then on the arrest slip, he's not the only officer that participated in this case. And then you know on the arrest slip and on the uniform citation there are other officers. Those are not the only officers that participated in the case. Name of witness, Sgt. K. Bell. Did we ever hear from K. Bell? And what was he a witness to? If he's a witness, he ought to be here. Name of witness, Sgt S. Bailey and K. Bell. If he's a witness, he ought to be here. You don't see the names of those other two guys on here as witnesses.

They want you to believe all dope is packaged for sale. Some of it is packaged for use. A lot of people are out there selling it, but there are a lot of people out there using it. I don't know what Mr. Hill was doing with it. That's not my job. But the question is have they proven his guilt beyond a reasonable doubt because he's not the one with the dope. He had the cocaine *[pointing to second defendant]*.

And then this big deal about the money being in small denominations. Well we only have five or six denominations. I know of ones, fives, tens, twenties, fifties, or hundreds. I use to think there were five hundred or thousands, but I think I must have been dreaming or something.

When we go to the bank and cash our checks, what do we get?

I am not going to ask for all hundreds. You ever go to McDonald's in the morning and try to cash a hundred, or go to somewhere in the middle of the day and try to cash a hundred. Oh, we can't cash that. Most people get fives, ten, twenties, and fifties.

Again, that's the chance to make a case where there is no case. Many, many reasonable doubts in this case. And [*referring to the instruction on reasonable doubt*] this applies to all of us. This instruction is required to be given in every criminal case. It's given in every criminal case. [*The prosecutor made so many objections that Hagan had to get a last slap at* him] He can't object to that because he knows I am telling the truth. It's given in every criminal case. Something is terribly wrong with this case. If you can render a verdict against my client on this kind of evidence, no one is safe. Today it's a drug case, but tomorrow it might be a robbery or a homicide case.

And then you know, I thought of some questions that the prosecution didn't answer, and so what I am going to do is read them, and maybe Mr. Dilger will answer them, and maybe he won't.

Question No. 1
Why for over five and one-half months has the Commonwealth represented by Mr. Dilger and the Jefferson County police department not done anything to tell us who are the material witnesses in this case?

Question No. 2
Why do some officers say they pulled in, and some say they backed in?

Question No. 3
Was this a sting operation or an entrapment that went bad and for some reason was compromised? I understand that it happens in police work, and if it was compromised, and they just don't wont to reveal the sources, then why not admit it, and dismiss the case against him and go on?

We come in here and we got police officers, not civilian witnesses, we've got police trained police officers, going to advanced evidence schools, advanced investigation schools, and they don't bring any notes, any books, and no folders here on this case. I don't know, and I can't remember.

And why not handle the evidence in this case with integrity so it is properly preserved, and send the pill bottle to the lab so it could be properly tested for fingerprints? So then there are no doubts, not reasonable doubts, but no doubts. If you got this pill bottle from the lab with the defendant's fingerprints on it, now what can I get up here and say about that? It was handled out there in the street the same way it was handled here in the courtroom. They didn't have any gloves here and no gloves there. The integrity of the evidence was compromised.

And why not take pictures of the scene so we can see the vantage point? And why tell us five and a half months later that somebody went back to the house and checked on the person that came to the car? But then when this officer gets on the stand, "Oh well, I might have told him that, but nobody went back to the house."

These two guys are riding as partners. [*pointing to two different officers*] He says somebody told him they went back. He doesn't remember who told him they went back. He says he did go back. He says he didn't go back. And if you two guys didn't go back, and you didn't see anybody go back, how do you know anybody went back? Well I don't know. Somebody told me that somebody went back to the house, that's very important in this case. And why weren't we given the benefit of the testimony of Officer Bell and Officer Bailey, listed on the arrest slip, listed on the arrest slip?

And finally, why are we in Jefferson Circuit Court, on next to the last day of August, trying a case where there is no evidence of trafficking or possession, as to my client, either as to the cocaine or as to the diazepam?

Why does he have to spend hundred and thousands of dollars defending himself, and practically losing his business. They still got his car on hold. Why? The car wasn't stolen and he wasn't driving illegally? You heard them say they called in his license and it was valid. He just didn't have it on him.

Ladies and gentlemen, I ask you to go back to the jury room and send a strong message to the Commonwealth. This case and this type of conduct will not be tolerated in Jefferson County, Kentucky. They are the people that are required to uphold the law, not to break the law and not to bend the law, not to change the rules, not to play fast with the rules. They are to be honest and candid, and to come in here and put you on a case, and enforce the criminal laws of this Commonwealth.

I ask you when you go back to that jury room don't to be

in a hurry. I know we have been here for two days. The decision you make today will follow this defendant the rest of his life. And I ask you not to make a hasty decision. As far as I am concerned, it wouldn't take you long to come to the conclusion that I have come to. But if it does, stay back there. Do not put yourself in a position of having to wrestle with "Well, did I make the right decision on this case, or I am not sure or I don't know."

Sometimes when you stand on principle you have to stand alone. And if that be the case here, then stand untill hell freezes over. Go back there and do what is right, and do not compromise with what is wrong. Thank You.

Case #10

Date of verdict:	August 31, 2000
Charges:	Trafficking in Controlled Substance First Degree Class C Felony
	Trafficking in Controlled Substance Third Degree Class A Misd.
Possible sentence:	5 to 10 years
	12 months in jail and/or $500 fine
Judge:	Hon. Geoffrey Morris Jefferson Circuit Court
Prosecutor:	Hon. Craig Dilger

Defendant's opening argument:	4 minutes
Defendant's closing argument:	18 minutes
Commonwealth's closing argument:	15 minutes
Reasonable Doubt used	6 times
Length of jury deliberations:	60 minutes

Was defendant a convicted felon?	NO
Did defendant testify?	NO

Verdict:	**NOT GUILTY***
	Trafficking First & Third
	GUILTY*Possession of Cocaine

*the defense admitted or conceded that the defendant was in possession of cocaine, since it had fallen from his pocket

SYNOPSIS

This co-defendant and defendant #1 in the previous case were both charged with Trafficking in Cocaine and Trafficking in Diazepam and Complicity.

On March 17, 2000 undercover veteran narcotics officers say they saw the defendant's vehicle back into a driveway and engage in what appeared to be a drug transaction. He pulled in and had a conversation with someone that came out of the house and pulled off. The defendant, a bricklayer, says he had just left work and was on his way to the bank to get money to pay the crew that worked for him

The officers decided to pull him over and asked everyone to exit the vehicle. . The defendant was searched and was found to have $843 in small bills and a cell phone. His two passengers were also searched. The second defendant had eight individually wrapped pieces of crack cocaine that dropped from his pocket or waistband, and in plain view, as the officers searched him. The cocaine had a street value of $250. A third passenger, who was in the back seat, and a possible informant, was let go.

The trial lasted a day and a half with neither the 1st or 2nd defendant taking the stand. This defendant, through his lawyer, admitted that the cocaine was his and that he had it for possession. The jury deliberated 60 minutes and found the 1st defendant **NOT GUILTY** of all charges, except no operators license (later dismissed as valid by the Court).

This defendant represented by the Hon. Paul J. Mullins was found **NOT GUILTY** of Trafficking in Cocaine and **NOT GUILTY** of Trafficking in Diazepam, but **GUILTY** of Possession of Cocaine, Schedule I (which he admitted during trial).

OPENING ARGUMENT
of Attorney PAUL J. MULLINS

    May it please the Court, Judge Morris, ladies and gentlemen of the jury. The defendant is 22 years old, and already he has some problems. He is addicted to drugs, and this time he was caught, and it has gotten him into trouble. You will hear that the crack fell out of his pocket. You will hear that it is 2.7 grams or about two sweet and low packets. We admit that. They found it in his pockets. It was his. Now how much is 2.7 grams of crack? Well if you would ask a crack addict, and you will hear this testimony, 2.7 grams of crack is enough to keep a crack addict high for a half hour. We are not talking about a whole lot. 2.7 grams is just two sweet and low packets.

    Prosecutors want you to believe that just because they found the crack on the defendant, he must have intended to sell it. But they will not prove anything to you other than he was in possession. They will not show you or tell you or explain to you, by any proof from the witness chair, that the defendant distributed cocaine to anyone or that he sold it to anyone, or that he received money in exchange for the cocaine from anyone, or that he manufactured cocaine.

    What the prosecution wants you to do is a lot of speculation to fill in the gaps they are going to leave. Ladies and gentlemen, in this country speculation and suspicion is not enough proof to convict people. Our standard is proof beyond a reasonable doubt, and they have to show you beyond a reasonable doubt that the defendant sold distributed or manufactured drugs. You will not hear any evidence proving that.

    When this case is over, I will ask you to return a verdict of guilty for my client only on possession because that is the only thing he stands before you guilty of. He is not proud of it. He's ashamed of it. He wants to get this case behind him. He wants to make sure he is the guilty person. When he got in the car, he did not advise his friend that he had drugs on him. He stands here in court today to admit to you that is the only thing he is guilty of.

    You will have to hold the prosecution to their job of proving that the defendant sold, transferred or distributed drugs. I want you to listen to everything I say because they cannot prove that. I will come back before you and ask you to find the defendant not guilty of trafficking in a controlled substance.

CLOSING ARGUMENT
of Attorney PAUL J. MULLINS

Paul J. Mullins, associate attorney, attended Waggener High School and graduated from the University of Kentucky with a major in English in 1993. He received his J.D. from the Brandeis School of Law, and was admitted to the practice of law by the Kentucky Supreme Court in May 1998. He joined Mr. Hagan's firm in 1998.

Ladies and gentlemen of the jury, this is the point at which my job as an advocate is about to end, and your job as jurors, the triers of fact, is about to begin. Ladies and gentlemen this is a case based solely on police speculation, contemplation, and suspicion. But none of that is proof. In this country we require the state to prove a defendant guilty beyond a reasonable doubt. That's why I love this country and what makes this country so great. Everyone is presumed innocent from the moment they walk in the door.

Now as I told you earlier, the state is going to ask you to return a verdict of guilty against my client for trafficking in a controlled substance. And I admitted to you my client was in possession of the controlled substance cocaine, not diazepam. I told you it fell from his pocket. We freely admitted that. What we dispute is that my client acted in complicity, or alone, to traffick in cocaine and peddle drugs to the community.

Now I sit back, and I look at this case and I wonder what has the Commonwealth proven to you? I would submit to you that the only thing that has been proven is in fact, as I told you in my opening, that the defendant, my client, was in possession of a controlled substance, cocaine. But they would have you speculate and believe as they do to make an inference that because he possessed cocaine, in proximity to others with money, that he must have been trafficking.

This is what I call a gap filler case. The Commonwealth has not met their burden, and has not proven my client guilty of trafficking. They are asking you to fill in the facts. They want you to leap and make an inference based on very little evidence.

In this country we don't convict people based on our suspicions. We convict them based on proof, proof from this witness chair, and proof from any and all exhibits that we present in court to you. I believe that reasonable doubt is sewn into the very fabric of this case. So I'd like to go over a some concerns in this case and point them out to you.

My first concern is about the house. The police officers are sitting in the neighborhood watching homes as they prepare to do, and not necessarily looking for certain individuals, and they see activity in the house. You would think that if they are sitting there watching houses, expecting something to go down at the house, that they would move in and freeze everyone in the house. Anyone who was in the house was let go. Any activity at the house was dismissed. Any evidence that could have been seized at the house was forgotten about. We don't know what was either left behind at the house, or any witnesses that were at the house. I don't know. The police officers admitted they don't know. The prosecutors don't know, so you don't know.

The second problem I have with this case is with regards to the handshake, the drug transaction that the police officer allegedly saw. He told you he didn't see money transferred. He didn't see any drugs transferred. He doesn't know if it was a handshake. He doesn't know if it was a meeting. He doesn't know if it was a greeting. He doesn't know what happened. He sees a gentlemen, a black male, whom he described, come from the house direction and walk over to the car and leave. He doesn't have any conversations that he can recall. He doesn't see anything transpire, other than the gentlemen walks over. There is a brief, what he calls a transaction, and a leave.

Now the reason why I have a problem with that is because it is entirely possible that the gentlemen could have come over to the car, said hello, had a brief conversation, "no, the person you are looking for is not here" and could have left. They don't answer those questions, because we don't have the person at the house here, or know the name, or have any identification from that person to figure out what he knew at the time of that transaction.

Now the police could have gotten a search warrant for the house and that throws up a red flag for me. If they are watching the neighborhood, watching all the homes, and no one gets a search warrant to search any of the houses, if in fact a drug transaction had taken place, the police could have taken thirty minutes of their time to detain everyone.

They had that power to go get a search warrant and search everyone at the house. Search the entire house, search the cars, search the yard, search the front yard, search the back yard, and search the trees. They didn't do any of that--they decided to dismiss it.

They trailed the car for about a couple of blocks trying to decide what they were going to do. Do we arrest the guy? Did you see anything? Well I don't know. What did you see? Well I don't know, but you better do something quickly, he is moving right along away from the scene of whatever we saw. Well let's just pull them over and see what we find.

So that's what they did. They pull him over and they get

everyone out of the car. They separate all of the defendants. And then they say, "Well we got some money over here. We got some drugs over here. Well let's call in the canine unit." And this is what I find very, very peculiar. The canine unit comes up to the car and he sniffs the seat. And they say "well we've got a passenger sitting here, we knew he had drugs." So yes, we got a hit right here. So then they walk over to the next seat, and they say, "well let's stick the money right here that we found on this passenger outside." Let stick it right here in the car, right next to where the drugs were, right next to where the person with the drugs were. Let's stick $843 right here. Let's let the dog smell it. Well you got a hit.

And then you heard Officer Hatchett testify that "well it really all depends on whether there is a hit or miss, whether or not there are drugs in the area, whether the wind is blowing right, whether or not the temperature is right." But the dog made a hit, there were no drugs, but the dog made a hit, but the dog made a hit.

Then he says, "Well we got another $600. We are going to take that money out of the car. We are going to take that money and stick it in another car. Let's let him sniff it over here." No hit. It's not in the car, it's over in a clean car where no drugs or nobody was sitting in the car with drugs. And he says, "well let's have him sniff that." Well there's no hit, so we got to let this guy go. He's got $600 bucks. He's been in a car with a guy with drugs on him, and what we consider a large amount of drugs. He's been in the car. But you know what, let's just let him go. Let's just get these two because this is the guy I want. I want this guy, I don't want this guy. Let's let this guy go. Let's let the guy in the house go, because we don't want him. We want this guy. That's exactly what happened.

Okay, so you take the money and stick it in the car where you already got a hit on the passenger side, and doors open on both sides. You got wind blowing in from one side, but the dog got a hit. I've got a problem with that. Why not take the money and stick it in a neutral place, just like you did the other money?

And then you wonder, well where is the money? Let's take the money and commingle it back into society. Put it in the bank and let's forget about it. Don't give them a chance to test it. We won't test it. We will just put it back into society, and let it get handled and forget about it. We don't need it. We are going to win this case on the strength of our dog.

I asked officer Hatchett, were the dogs always accurate. Could it be that this dog missed on the money, which is practically the only thing that they have to link my client with for drug trafficking. Could it be that the dog missed on the money, but hit in the same vicinity of the front seat where the drugs were in someone's pocket.

So we get to the drugs and the drugs were in my client pocket. The drugs fell out of his pocket. He admits it threw his counsel. And they say we saw a transaction, so there must have been a sale.

And then under cross-examination, we asked the officer "was it a buy, was it a sale, could it have been anything else." I don't know. It could have been a buy, and it could have been a sale. It could have been anything. I don't know. He doesn't know. Prosecutor doesn't know. I don't know. You[*referring to the jury*] guys can't know.

Nobody knows except the three people who were in that car. And one of them, who we could have put on the stand and asked, we don't know his name until we come to trial.

And our clients are not required to take the stand and admit it. And I don't want anyone to hold it against them. Well if they didn't take the stand, I guess they must have done it. That's not what the law says. You cannot hold the fact that our clients did not take the stand against them, and I don't want you to.

Now the prosecution may get up here and say, "well he had a very large amount of cocaine. He had eight pieces." Eight pieces of cocaine and that's what the evidence says. You got the officer up here who admitted cocaine is brittle and it breaks up. I showed him, I said "well it's powdery down here, what happened?" It must have got crushed a little bit during handling. Is that what it looked like when you got it, the first time you saw it. No, it's been handled and it's been crushed up a little bit. It didn't really look like that. But they presented it to you, and said its eight pieces of cocaine, and obviously with eight pieces, I guess he was selling it.

Remember back in voir dire when I asked you about a roll of toilet paper. If someone buys cocaine from another person, and they want more than one hit or more than one high, and they buy multiple amounts they are going to receive individual amounts. So if you buy eight pieces of cocaine because you want eight highs, or you want to get high over the weekend. While I detest that, and I think that is wrong, but that does not necessarily make an inference that you are going to sell all of that cocaine.

If you got eight cigarettes, it doesn't mean you are going to sell eight cigarettes. You might want to smoke one now. You might want to smoke one fifteen minutes from now. You might want to smoke all eight of them at the same time. It is not my job to prove to you that my client was not going to sell this cocaine. It's their job to prove that he was. And have they done that? I don't think so.

Then we have the diazepam. They want you to believe that he was in possession, that he exercised control and that he was selling it. We have the diazepam here. It has a specific label on it. It has a persons name on it. The police officers don't take the time to make a phone call and say "Pauline we got some pills down here, a prescription. Did you leave it in the defendant's car?" I left those in his car. I'm glad you found my pills. Its valium, its muscle relaxers, and my back has been hurting. I don't know, but it's their job to prove that to you, to rule out that possibility, but they didn't.

Now when you get back to the jury room, you will have these jury instructions in front of you. And you will get a definition for complicity, and it is going to be in the Instructions that you have to believe either #1, that the defendant was acting solely to distribute, transfer, sale, or manufacture drugs which they have not proven to you. Or you have to believe that he acted in complicity with Barry Yocum with the drugs, which they have not proven to you.

Now Barry Yocum's lawyer will get up here and defend his case. I won't do that. But what I will tell you is that Ted Harmon did not have any cash. If Ted Harmon made a sale, he would keep his own cash. The guy in the back seat with $600, that's his cash. Why would one person hold on to their own cash, and another person not hold on to their own cash? If you don't know that answer, you may have a doubt. But we are not here to speculate, to guess, to make assumptions, as to why people do things.

Sometimes the law is very clear, very harsh and very sterile. Sometimes fact situations cannot support a conviction. This is one of those cases. It doesn't matter what a person may believe transpired on March 17th. It matters what is proven and proven beyond a reasonable doubt. If you believe that the unknown person in the car with the gentlemen was somehow a person involved, and Barry Yocum was not, you cannot convict Ted Harmon of conspiring with Barry Yocum. The Instruction doesn't say that, and the law doesn't leave room for that.

Ladies and gentlemen I don't really know what the prosecution is going to get up here and say. I can only guess. But what I want you to do is, if you still retain your notebooks, when he is delivering his closing argument, make a list called what have they proven, and make another list of what they suspected, of what they believe is possible. Make those lists. And if your list comes up with items of what's possible, what's suspected and may have happened, you might have some reasonable doubts.

Again I'd like to thank you for your time and patience. This is the last opportunity I have to speak on behalf of the defendant. I don't get a second chance. When you go back to the jury room to deliberate, and are trying to reach a decision, remember everything I have said to you today. And when you do reach a verdict, reach a verdict that is first of all obvious. That he was in possession of cocaine, he does not deny that. As far as trafficking in controlled substance, you can look the prosecution square in the face and say, "this was an interesting case, but we do not believe you proved your case beyond a reasonable doubt. Regardless of what I may think of defendant #2, I cannot convict him, because I cannot see that you have proven your case beyond a reasonable doubt, that he was trafficking in cocaine or trafficking in diazepam. Diazepam is the only pill in that bottle, and because it is a prescription pill, it is illegal for anyone other than the person on the bottle to have it. We do not know if Pauline left that in the car or not.

  Please find my client not guilty of trafficking but only guilty of possession of the cocaine, and not the diazepam. Thank You.

CASE #11

Date of verdict:	April 30, 2002
Charge:	Assault First Degree, Class B Felony
Possible sentence:	10 to 20 years
Judge:	Hon. Thomas Wine, Jefferson Circuit Court
Prosecutors:	Hon. Mr. Robert Bohnert & Hon. Khalid Kahloon
Defendant's opening statement:	5 minutes
Commonwealth's closing argument:	15 minutes
Defendant's closing argument:	31 minutes
Reasonable Doubt used	19 times
Length of jury deliberations:	1 hour 20 minutes
Was defendant a convicted felon?	YES
Did defendant testify?	YES
Verdict:	**NOT GUILTY**

SYNOPSIS

The defendant was charged with a single count of Assault 1st for allegedly assaulting a former girlfriend at the Petersburg Motorcycle Bar at 1:00 a.m. The victim, Marilyn Blackburn, and her friends accosted the defendant and attacked him first when he left the bar. They pulled his new girlfriend out of the car. They drug and beat her, beat the defendant, and damaged the defendant's vehicle. Other people came out of the bar and joined in the fight. The fight got so big after it moved across the street, that the bouncers decided to close the club and call the police.

The victim testified that the defendant and his brother and other friends came over to her house after she got home, and pistol whipped her in the courtyard, while her father was watching from a balcony. This defendant, a convicted felon, took the stand and testified in his own defense. His girlfriend also testified. Several of the other females involved in the fight testified. The jury returned a verdict of **NOT GUILTY** on the charge of Assault 1st degree.

OPENING STATEMENT

Judge Wine, Mr. Bohnert, Mr. Khalid, ladies and gentlemen of the jury. You will hear evidence in this case about a fight. The prosecutor is correct. It took place on Friday December 17, 1999 at a place called the Petersburg Motorcycle Club out in Newburg at 4:30 in the morning. The fight was instigated and started by Marilyn Blackburn Phillips, Shakira Beeler, Mona Brown, Bereioca Tinsley, and three or four other females.

And it started, he's right, Shakira Beeler and Marilyn Blackburn got there together. They had been drinking. In fact, Ms. Beeler will tell you they drunk almost a fifth before they got there. So they were extremely drunk. He comes into the club with his girlfriend, Savannah Hayes. And yes, he knows these other women, and he may have been a boyfriend with one of the other women at one time.

He came into the club with his girlfriend. And there was a pool table in this motorcycle club. And you have to put money up and get into line, I guess, to play pool. And so when it was his turn, he had laid the money wherever it was supposed to be laid, he goes over to play pool, and Shakira Beeler says no you are not playing pool. It's my pool game this time. And she says, "Anyway, why did you bring that woman into our club." Now this club is the Petersburg Motorcycle Club, it doesn't even exist anymore. The building has been torn down.

Anyway she confronts the defendant and they have a few words. And he decides its time to leave. He leaves the club, along with Savannah Hayes, and another gentlemen that was with them, Marvin Goins. They leave the club and they go out to get into his Ford Explorer or Expedition. I don't know which one it is.

Savannah gets in on the passenger side on the front. He goes around to the driver's side, and Mark is going around to the passenger side rear. What happens? Three things happen. Number one, a bottle, a beer bottle, is thrown with violent force towards the windshield, and hits the windshield. Number two, Savannah Hayes, she is already in the car, her door is opened and she is pulled out of the car and beaten by two or three friends, of Marilyn Blackburn and Shakira Beeler. And what does Shakira Beeler do? As he sees what is happening and is going around that side to help his girlfriend, Shakira comes up and lays a hay maker on him. Just "bop" out of nowhere. And then comes Marilyn Blackburn, and it's like a tag team, a wrestling team, a relay match.

Well there are about five or six or seven females fighting him, and he is defending himself and fighting back. And then what happens? All of the people at this time are pouring out of the club and people are trying to break up the fight. The fight lasts for ten or fifteen minutes. At that point nobody bothers to call the police. People are trying to break it up. So at some point they get away, and they get in their car and get ready to leave. The other ones get away and go in their car and they are ready to leave. And what happens then?

Shakira Beeler, knowing that this man has been a friend to all of them, a friend to Marilyn Blackburn, a friend to Shakira, a friend to his girlfriend Savannah, she calls him on the phone and tells him, "Why don't you come over here so we can talk about what happened." And you might question, maybe he should or should not have went over there. He went over there, and his girlfriend she sits in the car.

He gets out of the car and goes into the courtyard and he sits there and talks. I'm not going to say talking, they are probably arguing. And they are probably loud, they are cursing, its 4:30 or 5:00 in the morning. And evidently some of the neighbors got wind of what is happening, and somebody decides to call the police. Somebody hollers out and says they are calling the police. What does he do? He gets in his car and leaves. Corey Brown is his brother, but Corey Brown was never in the club, and Corey Brown was never at her house. While he went over there to her apartment, he never went into her house.

When the police get there, she makes up a story about being pistol whipped. I don't know if she told the police, and you will see the report from the police and from the hospital, where she tells all these different and conflicting things about what happened.

Ladies and gentlemen you may or may not hear from the police officers in this case, because of course they only took the report. They were not there and they couldn't see what happened. They could only go by what they were told. All the defendant was doing was defending himself. He had a right to defend himself. He had a right to defend his girlfriend. These ladies jumped on him, and they were extremely drunk, and there were six, seven, or eight of them. And she did not give the police all of the information. If she had given the police all the information, the police could have done a more thorough investigation.

At the end of this case I'll be back up here, and I'll be asking you to find this defendant not guilty of Assault in the 1st degree. Thank you.

CLOSING ARGUMENT

Thank you your honor. May it please the Court, Judge Wine, Mr. Bohnert, Mr. Khalid, ladies and gentlemen of the jury, let me add my thanks for your service on behalf of myself and my client. The way we do juries in the United States this is our preferred method and this is the only method that we know. And a lot of times I don't think jurors get enough credit for the service that they perform.

Most stories have one beginning and an end. A trial has two beginnings and two endings. Because my job as defense counsel is about to end and their job as the prosecutors is about to end. And your job as jurors the fact finders in this case is about to begin.

And I pointed out to you when we did jury selection or voir dire that your job is simple. To listen to the evidence that comes from the witness stand, follow the Instructions of law given to you by the Court, apply the Instructions of law to the evidence as you have determined it, and then and only then do you render a verdict.

Now at the beginning of this case we asked you several things. We asked you whether you understood that the indictment was not evidence in this case. You said you understood that.

We asked you whether you understood that the burden of proof is on the Commonwealth and never shifts to the defendant to prove that this defendant is guilty of these charges beyond a reasonable doubt. We asked you whether you understood that the defendant comes into this courthouse and into this courtroom and still has the presumption of innocence until you retire and deliberate and reach a verdict.

And we asked you whether you understood that if the Commonwealth failed to prove to you its case beyond a reasonable doubt, and you returned a verdict of not guilty, that you are still following the law.

And the final thing you understood was that reasonable doubt is the standard, not preponderance of the evidence, not some lower standard. Reasonable doubt is the standard that we use in criminal cases to determine guilt or innocence.

This case can only be decided on two things, the testimony that came from every witness that came out of that chair and these Instructions of law as given to you by the Court.

Now as I indicated to you at the beginning, we would ask and the judge would give to you an Instruction on self-protection. I would like for you to turn to that page, number 4,[*Mr. Hagan reading*] even though the defendant might otherwise be guilty of Assault in the 1st degree under Instruction 1, or Assault in the 2nd degree under

Instruction No. 1A, if at the time he struck Marilyn Blackburn with a gun and punched and kicked her, he believed that Ms. Blackburn as then and thereabout to use physical force upon him or another, he was privileged, he was privileged to use such force against Ms. Blackburn, as he believed was necessary in order to protect himself or another against him

And he told you he was trying to defend himself and his girlfriend who had been attacked. It is undisputed. The evidence is undisputed that his girlfriend was attacked. He's trying to protect her. He's trying to protect himself. He was privileged. That means he's got a right. It's a constitutional right. We all have that right. That protection comes to this Courthouse with him and into this courtroom. That's a protection under both the laws of the Commonwealth of Kentucky, and that's a protection under the United States Constitution.

And then these Instructions, if you go to the next page, you've got some definitions there, #3 "serious physical injury." Well you've got one that says physical injury. There is no doubt that Ms. Blackburn sustained physical injury. There is no doubt that the defendant sustained physical injury. There is no doubt that all the other people in the fight evidently sustained some type of physical injury.

[Mr. Hagan reading] And then the next one, "serious physical injury" means physical injury which creates a substantial risk of death. Has any evidence come from that witness stand that the injury she sustained created a substantial risk of death? You did not hear from any medical providers. You weren't given any medical records. [Mr. Hagan reading] ...or which causes serious and prolonged disfigurement.

Was there any evidence from the witnesses that there was going to be prolonged disfigurement, [Mr. Hagan reading] prolonged impairment of health, or prolonged loss or impairment of the function of any bodily organ. You had one medical provider, which was a dentist. And he said he couldn't tell you even how she got the injury, whether it was a fist, or a pole, or whatever it was, he said he couldn't tell you.

And then when you go the next page, presumption of innocence. There it is again. And the second paragraph says you shall, you shall find the defendant not guilty unless you are satisfied from the evidence alone. Now not from any speculation, not from it couldn't have happened any other way, or it more likely than not happened this way, not from what probably happened, but from the evidence alone, and beyond a reasonable doubt that he is guilty.

And then it says if upon the whole case, if you look at this whole thing, put this whole picture in your mind, if upon this whole case, something doesn't fit, then you've got a reasonable doubt, and you must find him not guilty.

Remember the Commonwealth alone has to paint the complete

picture that this defendant is guilty beyond a reasonable doubt.

Now during my opening, I promised you we would show you several things. I told you that this was a bar fight that happened at the Petersburg Motorcycle Club, December 17, 1999. And that this fight was instigated and started by Shakira Beeler, joined in by Marilyn Blackburn, Mona Brown, Bereoica Tinsley and other people.

The defendant and his friends said no fight happened inside the club. That's undisputed, but after they decide to leave, what happens? All hell breaks loose outside. Savannah Hayes who is in the car with the door closed, she has the door opened, and she is drug out of the car onto the gravel pavement. She gets beat up. She gets her hair pulled out, and she has bruises and scratches.

And then the defendant who is coming to her aid, he gets pummeled by four or five people. And then other people joined in. And we also told you this fight lasted ten or fifteen minutes, and involved eight or nine or more people. But Ms. Phillips wants you to believe, there were only four people.

And then Shakira Beeler and the defendant, they were pushing and shoving, and somebody else was fighting with Savannah, and she was trying to break it up. Now that's what I promised I would show you. Now I ask you to judge whether I kept my promises.

Mr. Khalid said this case is about a bully and a terrorist. A woman who stands up to this bully is savagely and brutally beaten. These four pictures, all the physical evidence that you've got, and I am not, and I am not making light of her injuries, because she was injured.

But that's what happens when you take the law into your own hands and when you start a fight with drunken people. And then the prosecutor asks, "Well you just decided to show up." You knew they were at the club. So he shows up and they say it's our club and then Marilyn Blackburn she says she was coming to the aid of her friend. You don't come to the aid of a person who is the attacker or the aggressor. You don't have that right.

Her friend was the one who started it inside the club and continued it outside, Just like I asked her, "if you had stayed in the club, none of this would have happened." No. And her friends were the ones who decided to follow her out of the club. She tells her friends to come on. It's on.

Now if the police had done the proper investigation, guess who would be sitting here? Shakira Beeler, Mona Brown, Marilyn Blackburn, and Bereoica Tinsley and whoever else they could have found that was involved in the fight.

It is obvious that the Commonwealth has defaulted on the promises made to you during opening. Instead of honoring that promise, that promise has come back marked insufficient evidence.

And you know the scene; I don't have to go over the scene. What happened? They all get outside beer bottles are being thrown. Pop bottles are being thrown. The fight stops and then it move across the roadway. It continues. It got so bad that the club manager just decided to lock everybody out of the club.

Nobody bothers to call the police until it's all over, until a bunch of people are injured. There is no doubt and it is undisputed as to what Shakira Beeler said. Their witness, they called her. Who struck first? She struck him in the mouth first.

And then Mona Brown threw the bottle. "I may have hit Savannah one time." Nobody remembers how much they had to drink. Shakira says they had a fifth at the house, and then they continued drinking in the club.

And then you come to the Commonwealth's first witness. I believe that is one that even Shakespeare couldn't describe. One who claims to have been a witness, but she is no where listed by the police as a witness. The officer said Anthony Boyd was the person he listed down on the report.

But Mr. Bohnert stands right back over there behind that desk, and asked him one last time, "Are you sure" trying to jog his memory. He remembers it well. He had his report. Nettina Carter was not there. But she comes in the courtroom and wants you to believe otherwise. She might baby-sit for the woman, I don't doubt that. She was friends with the woman. I don't doubt that, but she was not there. Shakira says she was not there. She wants you to believe she was there.

And then she was the one that knew Anthony Boyd, and that he might have been a friend of someone next door. And Anthony Boyd is the one that Marilyn Blackburn says, "I don't know him. Oh maybe lived a couple of doors but he is in Chicago now." He is the same one that signed her out of the hospital, and she doesn't know him. Would you let a total stranger sign you out of the hospital?

Mr. Khalid asked, "Oh you know the difference between telling the truth and telling a lie" but she couldn't look at him, and identify him as the one who pointed at the woman that baby-sits for her.

And then she says she locked the door and called the police. But Marilyn says she went upstairs and her neighbor called the police. He didn't interview here because she wasn't there. I want you to judge her demeanor. He didn't interview her because she wasn't there.

And then Donald Phillips, Marilyn's father, comes in. And if you don't send him to the penitentiary for ten or twenty years on what Nettina Carter says, then send him to the penitentiary on what Donald Phillips says.

But Donald Phillips he says he was not present at the bar. He never saw the defendant come out of her apartment. He never saw him in her apartment. In fact when he saw him, he was standing there. And he didn't touch her in anyway.

Now she wants us to believe that they assaulted her in the apartment, and then they moved outside. Or as the prosecutor says, "They took her out of the apartment, and then they were outside down on the ground kicking her, and her father is standing looking over the rail. Now would a father stand there and let his daughter get the hell kicked out of her, while he's just standing there watching? He came in here and he swore to his oath. I believe he was truthful and honest with you. I respect him for coming in here, but he's not going to lie for his daughter. He didn't confirm any of her story, but the most important thing you heard him say and that was important. He didn't see the defendant touch her. Now if she was all this bloody mess, wouldn't he have come down and come to her aid?

The defendant is a terrorist, a bully. He's a terrorist because he walks away, tries to get away from what is going to break out, and tries to get in his car and leave. He's a terrorist and a bully because he tries to defend himself and his girlfriend. What would anyone of us have done?

If a girlfriend, a boyfriend, a sister or brother, a good friend of ours were attacked? You went into a club and you came outside and were attacked. Why did they follow him out of the club? There was no need for them to go out there. It was an argument, it had ended, just leave it and everybody go home. It is already 3 or 4 in the morning and most of them are drunk.

And then the prosecutor said during his opening "That she was beat savagely with the pistol." Does that look like a savage beating? To me it looks like what happens when you get in a fight and you lose. You are on the losing end of a fight. You get black eyes, a couple of stitches in your mouth, and you get a busted lip.

They called the police. And I believe that they were trying to set him up. They called him back over. There wanted him to come back so they could talk about it. Although they really called him because they wanted to call the police back over there, so they could blame it on him, because they were the instigators.

And they very well could have gone to jail, for criminal mischief for throwing a bottle at the car, assault for attacking and dragging Savannah out of the car, and attacking the defendant.

And then Marilyn Blackburn comes on the stand. She wants you to believe she had nothing to do with it. She is on the dance floor. She is drunk. She wants you to believe with all the fighting going on, she is trying to break it up and she gets popped.

She jumps into the middle of a fight, a fight started by her friend, a fight instigated by her friend. And then she says it was just a shoving match, just a little pushing and shoving match between the defendant and Shakira, and something else going on over there with Savannah.

And then she says she got hit in the back of the head with a gun. Now where is the evidence or the medical proof that she got hit in the back of the head with a gun? You would think that a gun would cause a least a bump, a bruise, a scratch, or a gash.

No evidence, but the prosecution wants you to guess, they want you to speculate, they want you to say it probably happened, it possibly happened, it couldn't have happened any other way, but no evidence beyond a reasonable doubt.

And then Marilyn she says she doesn't know Corey Brown. She knows both of them. She knows Kenneth Brown, she knows Corey Brown, but she says Corey unknown. Corey unknown, that's a nice name, Corey unknown. And then she doesn't give the defendant's real name. She gives the name Kenneth Brown.

Well why would she want to lie about these facts? Well she is involved in a fight instigated by a friend, started by a friend, in which several people got injured. They throw beer bottles, they yank the girlfriend out of the car, they beat the hell out of her, they pull her hair out, and they pull his hair out to the point that he can't wear braids anymore.

I want the twelve people that will decide this case to do me one thing. Think about if you've ever taken some tweezers and pulled a hair out of your nose or off your eyelids. It hurts, and I would submit to you that it hurt likes hell when somebody pulls a clunk of hair out of your head. And you are going to fight back. You are going to defend yourself. And then when she gets home they are back over there and the little argument or whatever starts again. The police are called. This would make a great story for television if it weren't so pathetic.

Why are we here today? Why are we in this courtroom Thursday, two days before Derby, why are we here? Because the police didn't do a proper investigation, because I guess nobody at the club would talk to them. And the Commonwealth didn't have the guts to dismiss the case. That's why we are here. That's exactly why we are here.

They want to shift the focus from the defendant. Nobody ever went and took out a warrant for Mona Brown for throwing a bottle. Nobody ever took out a warrant on anybody for pulling Savannah Hayes out of the car. And then Officer McNear said that he did no follow-up. He didn't talk to anybody else, Anthony Boyd, or Marilyn Blackburn.

And then you heard from the other three witnesses. Mona Brown of course she wants to say, "I didn't throw the bottle. Now I might have hit, I might have hit Savannah, but I didn't throw the bottle."

Everybody else says she threw the bottle. She wants you to believe she didn't throw the bottle.

And then Savannah Hayes, I asked Ms Blackburn, "You say you're the victim"? I think Ms Hayes is the victim in this case. She did nothing to provoke anybody. He did nothing to provoke anybody. No medical proof here. They just want you to guess.

First you come into the courtroom, and its Assault 1st degree, and now its either Assault 1st or Assault 2nd. So if you don't find him guilty under Assault 1st, where there is a serious physical injury, because you can't find any evidence of serious physical injury, then just go on and skip to the next page, and find him guilty of Assault 2nd, causing physical injury.

We are talking about a black eye. We are talking about a busted lip, a chipped tooth. Serious and prolonged disfigurement? Didn't go back to the doctor, went to the dentist and had a root canal. Serious physical injury? I don't think so ladies and gentlemen.

And I can't, as the prosecution said, "we cannot define reasonable doubt for you." But we can look at the evidence to see if there are some areas where you might have reasonable doubt.

And I submit to you that if you have those doubts, like I do, when you go back to that jury room, point out your reasonable doubts to your fellow jurors, whether it comes from something I said, something they said, [*pointing to prosecution*] or something you gained from that witness chair. Point out your reasonable doubts.

Doubt #1

No proof that the defendant intentionally assaulted this woman. He got into a fight with her and her *rowdies* at the club and that's where the fight ended. He defended himself and he defended his girlfriend, which he had a right to do.

Doubt #2

And she did not get beat savagely, as the prosecution wants you to believe. She didn't get beat savagely. He didn't beat her to a bloody pulp. He didn't beat her untill there was no life left in her. As he said, Shakira hits him first, and he turns around to swing and misses her, and then he gets hit on the other side. And then when he turns to look to see who's hitting him, he gets hit again. So it is like a relay team, a tag team, a wrestling match. And then there are other people in the club, they come out and they get involved. Men are taking sides, they don't know who started the fight, and people are just jumping in.

You know you got those little pads there, when the prosecution gets up here, just draw you a line, what have they proven on this side, and then reasonable doubt on this side.

And everything they say just when you got questions about it just circle it. Have they proven it beyond a reasonable doubt from the witness stand?

Doubt #3

And then the prosecutors said, "The bouncers just threw everybody out." The bouncers didn't take them out of there, they were leaving the club voluntarily. I guess the bouncers, after the fight started, and everybody was outside, they decided to lock the doors. That was the prudent thing to do. Didn't no bouncers... have you heard any evidence that the bouncers threw anybody out? If they should have thrown anybody out, it should have been the ones who started the fight.

Doubt #4

Netinna Carter is nowhere listed. She didn't talk to this officer. She said she talked to an officer and gave him the information. They asked her to come down and make a statement. Who was the officer? Where is the statement she gave?

And then she [*referring to Marilyn Blackburn*] goes down and takes out a warrant on him, but she doesn't tell them anything that happened at the motorcycle club. That's not important. It is not important. I would submit to you that it is very important.

It is important because there is a big fight, involving I don't know how many people. I am not going to sit up here and try to speculate and guess on how many people, I don't know how many people. Everybody except Marilyn says, it was a large number of people. Bottles being thrown, beer cans being thrown, beer bottles, somebody had a pole, somebody had a finger nail file.

It's not my job and it's not your job to solve this case. That job belongs with the Commonwealth of Kentucky. And I would submit to you that they did not solve it. And they did not bring proof into this courtroom that my client, the defendant, committed an assault on this woman beyond a reasonable doubt.

Don't fall for it. Don't go for it, because if you do, none of us are safe. If it could happen to him, it could happen to us. If the defendant hit her, and I believe he did hit her. I honestly believe he hit her, and he might have hit her more than once. But he hit her because he was trying to defend himself and defend his girlfriend.

If her teeth were broken, if she got a cut on her lip, she got a busted lip, her eyes were blackened, it is because she got into a drunken brawl with her girlfriends, and these people who tried to leave and resolve this situation peacefully.

The Commonwealth brought in all of these unnecessary witnesses. Donald Phillips, what does he add to the case? Netinna

Carter was obviously lying on the stand. They didn't bring in any medical proof. That would have been nice, wouldn't it? That would have been real nice, bringing in medical proof.

We would have known clearly what her injuries were. I don't know if her jaw was broken or her nose was broken. I know it was bleeding and bloody. That doesn't mean it was broken. By the evidence alone, remember, you can only judge it on the evidence that comes from that stand.

You know nature has endowed every species with the instinct of self preservation. A man has an absolute right to defend himself from great bodily harm, and to resist any attempt to inflict upon him personal violence. I don't think they will dispute that. He took defensive action proportionate to the apparent to the apparent and impending danger as he saw it.

The law of self defense has always been construed more strictly in our country because we have more to protect. We have more to defend. It is the apprehension of harm to you and the danger that justifies you acting in self defense.

Why should he wait? If he waited any longer, maybe somebody would have went over and picked up the beer bottle that Mona threw at the car, and cracked one of them over the head. Then we would have a different victim here, different charges against somebody else. Why did he have to wait? Wait until they pulled every piece of hair out of his head until he acted to defend himself

You might say well it was a woman. Well it was a woman. You are right, but she took the law in her own hands. Well of course nobody with any sense would agree with beating up a woman or beating up anybody for that matter. But don't take the law in your own hand and then come out and say, "I am the victim."

I say no, no, a thousand times no. Just as if our country were attacked tonight, we wouldn't wait until our cities were burning and our countryside was laid to waste. We would send armies forth and men to defend us. And just as a hunter is in the jungle, and he is looking for a tiger, and he sees the tiger spring he is not going to wait until the tiger springs, he is going to shoot the moment he sees the tiger.

But the Commonwealth wants you to send this man to the penitentiary on this kind of evidence and that would be a travesty of justice. But don't be in a hurry. I know there is a parade going on, and Derby festivities and all that, but don't be in a hurry. The decision you make today will last with him for the rest of his life.

By your verdict you will be saying to the Commonwealth, no this man is not a terrorist and he is not a bully. He had a right to defend himself. He had a right to defend his girlfriend, Savannah

Hayes. And you will be saying to the Commonwealth, you guys should have fully investigated this case before you brought it here and made us waste our time. And you will be saying to Marilyn Blackburn and Shakira Beeler, "that we don't live by the law of the jungle. We live by the laws that are instituted for all of our protection, and if a man or woman threatens your life you are privileged to act in self defense."

When we selected you as jurors, we said that we trusted you then and there, and we trust you now, that you will return a fair and impartial verdict and uphold the oath to which each of you swore. That you will listen to all of the evidence, without prejudice, without sympathy, even though I know she got hurt. You can't decide this case on sympathy, sympathy for him or sympathy for Ms. Phillips. You decide the case on the evidence.

And don't get caught in the position of having to wrestle later with what you do today. Because sometimes when you go back there in the jury room, you have to stand. And if you have to stand by yourself, then stand. Stand on principle. If you have to stand until hell freezes over, go back and do what is right and do not compromise with what is wrong.

I am proud to defend him in this courtroom today. I am proud to uphold the oath to which I swore. This man is not guilty. Thank you very much.

CASE #12

Date of verdict:	August, 13, 2002
Charges:	Theft by Unlawful Taking o/ $300, Class D Felony
	Persistent Felony Offender II
Possible sentence:	1 to 5 years
	5 to 10 years
Judge:	Hon. Stephon Mershon
	Jefferson Circuit Court
Prosecutor:	Hon. Kristen Poindexter
Defendant's opening argument:	10 minutes
Commonwealth's closing argument:	21 minutes
Defendant's closing argument:	31 minutes
Reasonable Doubt used	26 times
Length of jury deliberations:	37 minutes
Was defendant a convicted felon?	YES
Did defendant testify?	NO
VERDICT:	**NOT GUILTY**

SYNOPSIS

The defendant worked as a loader for a local hauling company. It was a Friday afternoon and the company was very busy. There were several loads that had to be sent out that day. Two trucks pulled into the dock at the same time, and this defendant was assigned to load it. He is seen loading it on one of several cameras at the dock area. He is then seen with the paperwork on the forklift.

The truck is allegedly loaded with over 350 Samsung Computer Monitors. The truck leaves and the monitors never turn up at the scheduled destination. The company begins to search for the paperwork and tries to track down the shipment. All employees that worked that day are contacted. This defendant is contacted at home, and says he doesn't know what they are talking about. On Monday morning the Jefferson County police are called in to investigate the alleged missing shipment.

The defendant, a convicted felon, is interviewed and subsequently arrested for the theft of the missing shipment. By the tie of trial the shipment and all paperwork were still missing. The 323 Samsung computer monitors were valued at over $500,000. This company ended up folding as a result of this missing shipment and other problems.

The defendant did not take the stand. The jury returned in less than two hours with **NOT GUILTY** verdict on the charge of Theft by Unlawful Taking over $300.00.

OPENING STATEMENT

May it please the Court, Ms. Poindexter, ladies and gentlemen of the jury, a half of million dollars of computers monitors come up missing on Friday June 11, a half of million dollars, 300 to be exact, 375 computer monitors belonging to Comp USA and destined for a truck stop somewhere in New Jersey or New York.

Out of the clear blue sky, gone, vanished, no monitors, no truck, no boxes with the monitors in them, no paperwork.

Well Comp USA is obviously going to be dissatisfied, the trucking company that is supposed to pick the monitors up is going to be dissatisfied.

Somebody is going to have to own up to where these monitors are at. Now they want you to believe that because he loaded the truck, and they've got video tape, and they've got charts, just because he was the last one to load the truck, and he may have violated some company procedures, that he committed the theft.

But ladies and gentlemen, we don't march every employee into the courtroom who violates a company procedure, and charge them with a half million dollars of stolen computer monitors.

The evidence will be in this case that this company, which is now out of business, as a result of this loss and of other things, had no security guard. I can just go over in a truck, and I can drive up there, and if I've got the right order number, I can pull in and up to the loading dock.

And now they want to say they got cameras, cameras don't work half of the time. Supervisors turn the cameras off for their own benefit. That's what kind of evidence you are going to hear. You are going to hear evidence of sloppy management, sloppy procedures, and procedures that are not effective. It's not his job to check the driver in. The driver comes up, rings the bell, and somebody from the office is supposed to get the paperwork, and then assign somebody to load the truck.

They don't have any procedures for writing down even the license number on the truck. Now if you knew the license numbers on he truck, you might be able to trace the truck, and find out what happened to a half million dollars of Comp USA computer monitors. No license numbers. The evidence will show that nobody writes down the description of the truck. Nobody gets from the driver his drivers license. You know, just ask him to take his drivers license out, and that way we can confirm that he is the right driver that is supposed to pick up the truck. But nobody asks the driver for a driver's license.

So once again, anybody can just go get a truck, and bring the truck up to the dock. There is no fence. We are dealing with millions of dollars worth of equipment that is coming in and out, and yet it's not safeguarded to protect the people that it's ultimately going to. No fence, no security guard, and no cameras. And then at the front office, everybody can go into the front office, the loaders, the supervisors, the drivers.

What kind of company is this? But they want to blame one person, because he is the last person to load the truck. And they call him on a Friday evening or Friday night. He got off work. I don't know if any of you have ever packed or loaded, or been in that kind of business, that's a hard job. So he went and got a beer. And that's not against the law, as long as he wasn't drinking and driving.

He goes and gets a beer, and they call him, and he tells them or they ask him about loading trucks. He may have forgotten how many trucks he loaded that day. They say it was a very busy day. So evidently everybody was loading a lot of trucks that day. He goes in the next day and he cooperates with them. He tells the police, "You can go to my house and search if you want to." They don't go to his house and search. If we find one computer at his house, or we find a piece of paper, we might be on the trail of a half of million dollars worth of computers.

I don't believe the evidence in this case will show, or they will prove to you, beyond a reasonable doubt, that he defendant was involved with taking the truck. Well who is he in complicity with? Well they say it's an unknown driver. Nobody gets a description of the driver. Nobody gets a description of the truck. All we have is that a truck is missing and somebody's going to pay. At the end of this case, I'll be back up here again, and I'll be asking you to return a verdict of not guilty.

CLOSING ARGUMENT

May it please the Court, Judge Mershon, Ms. Poindexter, Mr. Bohnert, Detective Burks ladies and gentlemen of the jury, first of all on behalf of myself as an officer of the Court and my client, I would like to thank you for your jury service. What you as jurors do is very much appreciated. It is the only system known in the world that has worked for as long as it has, and it's the only way we have to determine guilt or innocence under our criminal justice system

It's very important that you listen to what I say, because I am the last voice that will speak on behalf of this defendant. We don't get to go back and forth, like we do during the jury questioning. When I set down, I can't stand up anymore and refute anything they might say. And I don't know everything that they might say

It's important you listen as I am speaking on behalf of my client and the defendant. This case is a search for the truth. It is a search for the truth. This is where my job ends. The judge's job ends. The prosecutor's and police officer's job ends, and your job begins. Your job and your task is simple, to be fair, to do justice, to do the right thing in this case.

You are here to determine just from the evidence alone, that came from this witness chair, just from the evidence, whether the Commonwealth has convinced you beyond a reasonable doubt that defendant committed the offense of Theft by Unlawful Taking of property with a value of over $300 on June 8, 2001, and belonging to Ryder Logistics. That's your job.

And at the beginning of this case we went over several fundamental principles of criminal law with you. Now at the beginning of this case we asked you several things. We asked you whether you understood that the indictment was not evidence in this case. You said you understood that.

We asked you whether you understood that the burden of proof is on the Commonwealth and never shifts to the defendant, to prove that this defendant is guilty of these charges beyond a reasonable doubt. We asked you whether you understood that the defendant comes into this courthouse and into this courtroom and still has the presumption of innocence, until you retire and deliberate and reach a verdict.

And we asked you whether you understood that if the Commonwealth failed to prove to you its case beyond a reasonable doubt, and you returned a verdict of not guilty, that you would still be following the law.

And the final thing you said you understood was that

reasonable doubt is the compass, not preponderance of the evidence, not some lower standard. Reasonable doubt is the standard that we use in criminal cases to determine guilt or innocence, of each and every offense for which the defendant is charged.

This case can only be decided on two things, the testimony that came from every witness that came out of that chair, and these Instructions of law as given to you by the Court.

The Court has instructed you, and I want to go over that Instruction No#3. I think I blew it up [*referring to* chart] here a little. Instruction No. #3 says the law presumes a defendant to be innocent of a crime, and the indictment shall not be considered as evidence or as having any weight against him. And you shall…it's a mandatory word, shall, you shall find the defendant not guilty unless you are satisfied from the evidence alone, and beyond a reasonable doubt. Not from well he's probably guilty. Not from, well there is a strong suspicion of guilt. Not from, well it couldn't have happened any other way. He is the last one to load the truck, so he must have stole it. That is not evidence beyond a reasonable doubt.

This is a high standard of proof, beyond a reasonable doubt. If upon the whole case, if after you look at all of these circumstances, and all the evidence that's in here, and if upon this whole case, you have a reasonable doubt that he is guilty, then you shall find him not guilty.

And the fact that the defendant is not compelled to testify, and the fact that he did not testify, cannot be used as an inference of guilt and should not prejudice him in any way. The Commonwealth alone has to paint the complete picture in this courtroom for you to convict the defendant beyond a reasonable doubt of this charge. And ladies and gentlemen, it is not my job, it is not the judge's job, it is not your job to determine what happened to 375 monitors belonging to Ryder Logistics.

Now as a citizen, all of us should be concerned when a company and a business lose that type of equipment and that type of money. But that's not our job. That job belongs to the police department and to the Commonwealth Attorney.

Now as we pointed out to you at the beginning, we can't define reasonable doubt, but we can look at the evidence that came in, and see if there are areas in the evidence alone, from the evidence alone, as it says, from the evidence alone, areas where we can find some reasonable doubt

And I would submit that you don't need five, ten, or twelve. One single solitary reasonable doubt in this case is enough for you the find the defendant not guilty. And I brought another chart in here.

Reasonable Doubt #1.

The master tape from the eight cameras at Ryder Logistics on June 8th. Why didn't we have in evidence the master tape? We had a composite, something that was put together by a security company. We don't even know what security company put it together, or under what conditions they put it together, or, if Mr. Kalvin Huggins was sitting there, when they put it together. We don't know that. We don't know what quality standards were used. We don't have the tape. They gave you a snippet. Now is that a search for the truth?

Reasonable Doubt #2

The daily log sheets from 6/8/2001 from Ryder Logistics. They might say that's not important. It's very important because it might show us who signed in and who signed out that driver that went to the dock and got those computers. Very important and a search for the truth remember.

Reasonable Doubt #3

Company incident reports. We didn't even have a company incident report regarding what the company found from its own internal investigation. Now wouldn't you think that's important? I would, very important, but not in evidence.

Reasonable Doubt #4

Employees sign in and sign out sheet. Well they say, "No that's not important, employees sign in and out on the computer." Well that might determine who all was there when the shipment first came up missing, when it was loaded, or when it left. We don't know who was there, only by the people that came in. One lady says she wasn't there she left at 12: o'clock.

Kalvin Huggins wants us to believe he left to go to a meeting on one of the busiest days. Remember that Friday was a very busy day. They had some hot shipments had to go out. That lady came up on the stand and says, "Hot shipments mean ASAP, everybody drop what you are doing, and get these shipments out"--but no proof.

Reasonable Doubt #5

Copies of the company's written procedure for the employees to follow. That's a nice chart, prepared by the Commonwealth, but remember ladies and gentlemen, that's not the company's chart. The Commonwealth prepared that chart for this case. Where is the company's written procedures, that all employees are bound to follow, and which we now know were often not followed by many employees?

But of course Kalvin Huggins wants us to believe that everybody followed procedures all of the time. But even at the end when they brought him back on during rebuttal, and I asked him ,did all employees always follow procedures? And he had to admit, no.

And then you know, he walks in and brings this big binder, and I am thinking at some point that he is going to pull something out relating to this case. No reports, no notes, no documents, no other employees from the company, the company is out of business. And I asked him, "What did you bring with you to this trial?" "What I was supposed to bring, myself."

Reasonable Doubt #6

Seven missing witnesses. Now let's talk about that. Chantel Williams worked up in the front office. She wasn't called to testify. Once again, that's not my burden. I could call all of those witnesses but that's not my burden. That burden belongs to the commonwealth.

Scott Rand, now he is important because his office is where the computer monitors were. We might get some more information about this tape they put together, or this master tape that we have never seen from Scot Rand. But he didn't come in.

Randy Thompson, the Area Safety Manager, he could have come in and briefed us on what the security procedures were. What was in place. What was working. What was not working. Evidently something was not working. Huggins wants us to believe that everything is working, but right after this happened, he told you they had to go get $6000 worth of security equipment to take care of problems that the company was having

Brandon Hawkins, he is supposedly the one that picked the order the night before. Kevin Dennis, supervisor. William Graham, 2nd shift supervisor. None of these people brought in as witnesses, not one. And then they said they made an adjustment in the computer to adjust the computers that were missing, but we don't have any documentation of that.

A "search for the truth" by the Commonwealth. Seven witnesses missing. And then somebody said that the defendant gave false information when he applied. Did they ever prove that to you?

Now Josh wants us to believe that two trucks arrived and were required to be loaded at the same time, which was in between the shift change. Now who gave the order to load both of those trucks at the same time, which was a violation of policy regarding loading during shift change? Now who gave that order to load those trucks?

I have been around here a long time, and when the shift changes at the jail nothing happens. You can't go visit a prisoner, you can't get information, nothing. You can't get anything, everything stops.

Here is one prime example to prove that the company procedures were not being followed. Josh says we can load trucks up to 2:50 p.m., but Mr. Huggins says no, the cut off is at 2:30 p.m.. You will remember the testimony. I don't have to go over all the testimony because you have been very attentive, and I believe you have listened to all the testimony.

And then the security system that Kalvin claims and says is okay, and that they had to pay $6,000 for. And the camera system that is supposed to safeguard all of these companies precious and valuable inventories, Best Buy, Dextra, CompUSA, and Samsung. Nobody's monitoring the cameras. You've just got cameras up there, and nobody is monitoring them.

And now I thought about this last night, couldn't sleep, so I just got up and thought about the case. If Josh was loading the truck at the same time the defendant is loading the truck, why wasn't he on the video? He couldn't even tell me which dock he was loading the truck from. Now if the cameras are supposed to cover all the areas except #18 or #19, why wasn't Josh on the video?

You know then they say the cameras are moving around every four seconds. Nobody else, in fact nobody else is loading the truck other than the defendant.

And then they said they brought the trucks back and checked them, but we didn't get any records of what trucks they checked. No list of what drivers they brought back, no list of what shipments. We brought the trucks back. And then I asked him, "Did you have the cameras on." No. Well how do you protect the integrity of a company's merchandise if you don't record who is going back to check, to make sure they got the right shipments?

And of course they keep saying he didn't follow the policies, and we have determined from all of the fact witnesses that many of the policies weren't even his responsibility. How do you put responsibility on him, and say he didn't follow them, when it wasn't his responsibility to follow them. Log in the driver in and out, assigning the door, assigning somebody to load the truck.

Ladies and gentlemen, I believe all of these areas create reasonable doubt. And if you have doubts, whether it comes from a question I asked, something I said, or something you picked up on, point out to your fellow jurors what reasonable doubts you have about this case.

And the Commonwealth's witness, Detective Burke says, "This is not a murder case" No it is not a murder case, ladies and gentlemen, but I am treating it as the most important case I have ever tried, and it is merely a theft case.

No it is not a murder case, but do we lessen our standards as to this defendant because it is not a murder case? Do we compromise the integrity of the investigation because it is not a murder case? Do we trample the very meaning of our constitutional protections and safeguards because it is not a murder case? I don't think so, not in the

United States of America, not in the Commonwealth of Kentucky.

And Kalvin Huggins, he is not going to come in here and say that he gave computers away, or that he put computers in the wrong place. Did you expect him to come in here and admit that? No, I didn't. And then he testified and then he left. And then he testified this morning, and where is he? If I was Kalvin Huggins, and I was the Logistics Manager or Facility Manager for Ryder Logistics, I would be concerned about what happened in this case to my company's computers. I would certainly be concerned, and I would be here, and you would think some of the other people from Ryder would be here.

And then Josh Waddell, I think he testified honestly. He said he didn't know if the defendant gave him the papers or not. If he admits that the defendant gave him the papers and they are lost, his job is on the line too.

It is obvious that the Commonwealth has defaulted on the promise it made to you that this trial was "a search for truth" Instead of honoring or keeping that promise, the Commonwealth has given you a bad check, a check that has come back marked "insufficient evidence."

Yes there is evidence in this case. Yes there is evidence in this case, evidence that demands a verdict of not guilty. The writer *James Baldwin* said, "*The moment we break faith with one another or with our promises, the light goes out, the sea engulfs us.*" And I believe the light has gone out on the Commonwealth, as far as this case is concerned. It would be a travesty to convict someone on this kind of evidence.

And that is why those constitutional safeguards are there; presumption of innocence, defendant does not have to testify, burden of proof, reasonable doubt. That's why they are there, to protect against this kind of…what's happening in this courtroom.

We have been in here for two days. And let me point out this question to you. We have been here for two days. Do we really even know that the shipment is stolen? They [*referring to 375 Samsung computer* monitors] could be sitting in a warehouse in New Jersey, Indiana, Florida, or California. They could be sitting back in somebody's warehouse.

Don't you think if 375 monitors are missing, even if they sold them on the street, isn't it reasonable that somebody would have taken a monitor to a repair shop, and a serial number would have been traced? Especially with thieves, they deal with pawn shops all the time. And police check pawn shop details all the time and check serial numbers. So do we really even know if we have got a theft here? I only know that the monitors and the paperwork are gone. And there were a lot of people at Ryder Logistics that had just as much access to those monitors as the defendant.

If Josh Waddell had been the last person to load that truck

and the paperwork came up missing, guess what? Josh Waddell would be sitting here today.

If Cedric Nelson had been the last person to load that truck and the paperwork came up missing, guess what? Cedric Nelson would be sitting here today. It's just convenient to just pick the last person that loaded the truck. But that's not evidence beyond a reasonable doubt.

And no I'm not going to call it a cover-up. I am not going to call it playing flimsy with the evidence. I am going to call it reasonable doubt, because that's what it is.

When you go back to that jury room, or when the prosecution gets up here, of course they are going to say that the defendant is a wonderful, well-liked and respected employee, what else could they say about him? They didn't have anybody any person that they could bring in here that would say anything different. Not one person, not even Kalvin Huggins. He was a well-liked, well respected person. He did his job. Did he always follow procedures? Evidently when it got busy, it got a little slack for nobody followed the procedures, including Kalvin Huggins.

But you don't see Kalvin Huggins on trial, you don't see anybody but the defendant, because he is the one that loaded the truck, if he even loaded that truck.

Now from the evidence that they put on that screen, and I'll try to put it on this screen, do we even know which truck he was loading? I couldn't say which truck it was. I couldn't see any description on the truck. Do we even know which monitor? I couldn't see no name on the monitors. I don't know which monitor, Slim Line monitors, big monitor. I don't know what size or what name monitors, nothing.

That's why they called it a search for the truth. They don't know, I don't know, and if they don't know, and I don't know, how can you possibly know? But they want you to convict him of Theft by Unlawful Taking.

They asked lot of hypotheticals. It's easy to make a hypothetical. That's the first thing you learn in law school, about how to put together a hypothetical. Ladies and gentlemen, we are not here to deal in hypothetical. We are dealing with a live human beings life and liberty. We are not here to deal in hypotheticals, and what might have happened, or what could have happened, or it couldn't have happened any other way, or it must have happened this way. That's not proof beyond a reasonable doubt.

When they get up here to make their closing, whoever does it [*there were two assistant Commonwealth attorneys sitting on the case*], just take a little sheet of paper and draw a chart; what they have proven on the left, or what they want you to guess at, surmise at, or speculate on, on the right side.

Now ladies and gentlemen, I consider this case as very important. I don't consider this case as not important because we don't have television cameras and newspaper reporters. I consider this case as the most important case I have ever tried or ever will try, because a person's life and liberty hangs in the balance based on your decision.

And I know it is Friday afternoon and everybody wants to go home, and do whatever they want to do for the weekend. But when you go back to that jury room, stand. If you have to stand, stand alone. Stand until hell freezes over. Go back there and do what is right, and do not compromise with what is wrong. And I believe that you will believe, as I believe, that they have not proven his guilt beyond a reasonable doubt. Thank you ladies and gentlemen!

This Instruction should always be read to the jury or blown up on a chart for them to read.

PRESUMPTION OF INNOCENCE INSTRUCTION

The law presumes a defendant to be innocent of a crime and the indictment shall not be considered as evidence or as having any weight against him. You shall find the defendant not guilty unless you are satisfied from the evidence alone and beyond a reasonable doubt that he is guilty. If upon the whole case you have a reasonable doubt that he is guilty, you shall find him not guilty. The defendant is not compelled to testify, and the fact that he did not testify cannot be used as an inference of guilty and should not prejudice him in any way.

TIDBITS FOR USE IN YOUR CLOSING ARGUMENTS

ATTACKING POLICE INVESTIGATION

This was not a shoddy or sloppy investigation. There was no investigation. One set of photos. We've got six incidents and one set of photographs. No interviews of the area residents, or the people that maintain the beautiful cemetery next door. No dates on any of the rights waiver forms. No dates on many of the statements. No locations and no times.

BURDEN OF PROOF

At the beginning of this case when we questioned you, we asked you whether you understood certain things. One was that the burden of proof is always on the Commonwealth. The burden is never on the defendant. We don't have to prove anything. The burden always has been, still is, and always will be on the Commonwealth.

I would submit to you that in this case the Commonwealth has not painted the full picture. It is not your job to determine who stole a lawnmower from the City of Louisville on or about June 3. Your job is simply to determine, if from the evidence that's been presented in this courtroom over the last few days, the Commonwealth has satisfied its burden of proving to you beyond a reasonable doubt that it was this defendant that took that particular lawnmower

The Commonwealth, as we told you at the beginning of this case, has the burden of proof. We don't have to prove that he didn't do it. We don't have to prove anything. We didn't have to have him take the stand. He elected to take the stand and tell you what happened out there on July 31. They have to prove it and they have to prove it beyond a reasonable doubt.

Finally when you say to the Commonwealth at the conclusion of the case, Ms. Guilfoil, Mr. Hickey, and the officer, "you have not met your burden, you are still following the law. Just as if the case was clear and simple and the proof was here, you'd be following the law if you convicted them. So don't think that by returning a verdict of not guilty, you are not following the law. You are still following the law.
CHALLENGE TO THE JURY TO FIGHT FOR MY CLIENT

Five or six years from now I want you to look back on this day and say, "I know I did what was right in that case. I went back there and I didn't rush to judgment. I listened to my other jurors. I expressed my own opinions. I stood on my own convictions. I ask you to go back there and do what is right in this case.

CHALLENGE TO THE JURY & REQUEST FOR POSSIBLE HUNG JURY

Don't put yourself in the position of having to wrestle with this later and question whether you did the right thing. Sometimes when you take a stand and stand on principle, you have to stand alone. And if that be the case, so be it. Stand until hell freezes over. Go back there and do what is right and do not compromise with what is wrong.

COMMENT ON DEFENSE' LACK OF WITNESSES & EXHIBITS

As I indicated to you during the opening, we didn't have many witnesses. The Commonwealth always has more witnesses than the defense. But there are two important witnesses that have been in this Court the whole time. Number one is common sense and number two is human nature.

Now the prosecutor may stand up here and paint you a picture, well its just a matter of whether you believe him or whether you believe him. And if you believe him, he's guilty; if you believe him, he's not guilty. And I would submit to you it's not that simple.

COMMENT ON DEFENSE PROMISES

At the beginning of this case, I promised you that I would be fair with you. I gave you a promissory note. And I told you that there was no evidence here, other than what this child said that my client did anything to this child. No medical evidence. No evidence of any other witness. No evidence of any other allegations. I believe we kept that promise.

And we haven't tried to shift any blame here. And I can't say if somebody has messed with this child or not. But I can tell you there has been no medical proof that anybody messed with this child, and there certainly hasn't been any proof other than the one word of that child, that she was messed with by the defendant.

COMMENT ON LYING WITNESSES

Ladies and gentlemen, I'd say to you that these witnesses are not believable. If they would lie about one thing, they would lie about another. And I ask you to completely disregard their testimony. To convict somebody and send them to the penitentiary, you need truthful and credible evidence that comes from witnesses that don't have a motive to lie, that don't have a motive to change their story, that don't have a motive to change dates or to conveniently forget dates. They are forgetting dates. They are forgetting times. They are forgetting places. They are forgetting amounts. All of the critical things you need to decide this case. All of these witnesses seem to forget.

COMMENT ON PROSECUTION PROMISES

Now the Commonwealth made you some promises at the beginning of this case, some promises I believe were not kept, and I want to remind you of some of those.

CROSS EXAMINATION & OBJECTIONS BY DEFENSE

Now we also asked you whether you understood that it would be necessary for us to object and to vigorously cross-examine the witnesses. And that's our job as lawyers. That's the oath to which we swear. And that you wouldn't hold it against our clients, if you didn't like something we did, or if we objected too much, or you thought we cross-examined a witness too vigorously.

EXPLAINING TO THE JURY THAT AN ACQUITTAL IS FOLLOWING THE LAW

You [*referring to the jury*] further indicated that you understood and that we believed you that if the evidence justified an acquittal or if the evidence justified a verdict of not guilty that in so determining that verdict, if the evidence warranted it, that you would also be following the law.

INSTRUCTIONS OF LAW & REASONABLE DOUBT

So when you go back there and take these Instructions and Instruction #6 has that instruction in there. You might just want to write, so you don't forget it, you might want to write over the instruction in intentional murder, reasonable doubt still applies, It still applies as to wanton murder. It still applies as to manslaughter in the 2d degree, and it still applies as to reckless homicide. It still has to be beyond a reasonable doubt.

INSUFFICIENCY OF THE EVIDENCE

It is obvious that the Commonwealth has defaulted on the promise they made to each one of you, as far as this defendant and the other five defendants are concerned. Instead of honoring the promise they made to you, they have given you a bad check, a check that has come back marked "insufficient evidence" and not evidence beyond a reasonable doubt.

PRESUMPTION OF INNOCENCE & INDICTMENT

The presumption of innocence means that he is presumed innocent until he's proven guilty. And the indictment has no weight means that you can't use it in your deliberations to determine guilt or innocence.

We also asked you whether you understood that the presumption of innocence comes into this courtroom with this defendant and follows this defendant throughout the trial. He is presumed innocent until you go back and deliberate and return with a verdict.

REASONABLE DOUBT

Ladies and gentlemen of the jury, all twelve of you, you cannot convict the defendant on conjecture. You cannot convict him on the belief that he might have done it. You can't convict him on speculation. It's not enough to say he's probably or possibly guilty. That would violate all concepts of decency and fairness.

But these Instructions say that you must be satisfied from the evidence and the evidence alone, and beyond a reasonable doubt. Not from inferences, not from
hunches, not from guesswork. Not from a hunch "well if the cemetery was damaged, there is no other way it could have happened, they must have done it, but from the evidence alone and beyond a reasonable doubt. That's the compass or the star that has to guide your deliberations.

If upon the whole case you have a reasonable doubt, you shall find him not guilty. You shall find him not guilty. If you look at this whole case, and it springs reasonable doubt up in your mind, then look at those doubts. Point those doubts out to your fellow jurors. Let them know where you have doubt at in this case.

Ladies and gentlemen, suspicion is not proof, suspicion is not proof. If you have doubts about this case, like I do, when you go back to that jury room, I want you to point out those doubts to your fellow jurors. Show your doubts about this case to your fellow jurors

And finally you said that you understood that the amount of proof that is necessary to convict a person in a criminal case is a very high standard and that is proof beyond a reasonable doubt. And that proof, proof beyond a reasonable doubt, has to come from the Commonwealth's side alone. Not from this side, but from this side.

SELF DEFENSE ARGUMENTS *(for assault cases)*

The Commonwealth suggests you tell the defendant that he must go to the penitentiary for ten to twenty years because he wanted to defend himself.

The defendant's only intent was to stop David Wayne Stringer and that's what he did. And by your verdict you will be saying to this defendant that what he did was in self defense. And you will be saying to David Wayne Stringer that we do not live by the law of the jungle.

SHORT TRIALS

Now this case didn't take very long as most cases do. Most cases up here take two and three days. It didn't involve many witnesses. You usually have thirty or forty witnesses and ten or twenty exhibits. This case didn't take very long. But I don't want you to take it from the length of the case or from the brevity of it, that it's not an important case. It's a very important case.

SYMPATHY FOR MURDER or ABUSE VICTIM

And no, I'll say it again and again. Stephan Rudolph did not deserve to die like this. Whether he kicked over a table in the club, whether he was drunk, whether he was busing balloons, he did not deserve to die this tragic death. A precious human life was taken, but the problem is that the Commonwealth has not proven this case to you beyond a reasonable doubt.

WHEN PROSECUTION PUTS ON UNNECESSARY WITNESSES

The Commonwealth has put on numerous witnesses trying to make a case where there is no case.

GLOSSARY OF LEGAL DEFINITIONS

acquittal...what an accused criminal defendant receives upon a finding of not guilty. by a jury, or if the judge finds the defendant not guilty, or if the prosecution determines the case should not proceed any further

alford plea...a plea sometimes allowed in federal courts and some states courts in which a defendant is allowed to plead guilty but, at the same time maintain his/her innocence. It still results in what is the equivalent of a guilty plea

allen charge...a charge to a jury that is unable to reach a verdict to try harder. It may be prohibited in some states because of the feeling that it requires holdout jurors to surrender to the other jurors, even if they have doubts

assault...intentionally cause physical injury or serious physical injury to another person. Some states have varying degrees such as assault 1st, 2nd, or 3rd degree, assault, and/or assault with a deadly weapon, etc.

burden of proof... the standard in a criminal case that the prosecution or the state has of proving the defendant guilty beyond a reasonable doubt as to each and every element of the offenses of which he/she is charged

challenge for cause...the party's right in a criminal case to request that a juror be rejected because of some bias, prejudice or inability to be fair, or for some other legally sufficient reason that the juror should not be a juror in said case

circumstantial evidence...evidence that is introduced in a trial that does not come from what a witness saw or heard directly

citation...written notice to appear in court for the commission of some minor crime. Is often used instead of arrest. Sometimes the person may be allowed to respond by mail

closing argument...also called closing statements, the final argument or summation by the attorney for both the prosecution and the defense in a criminal case. Usually the defense attorney will go first, followed by the prosecution, but in some jurisdictions the prosecution will go first, followed by the defense counsel, and then the prosecution can again respond to the defense' argument

compromise verdict...a decision of a jury based on some jurors voting against their beliefs in order to break a deadlock and to achieve a verdict

credit for time served...the period of time a person has been in jail awaiting trial , unable to post bail, or awaiting sentencing, and for which they are usually given credit against any final sentence by the judge

cross examination...examination or asking of questions by the other side or by the party that did not call the witness

deadly weapon...any weapon capable of causing death or serious physical injury

defendant...the person before a court and charged with a crime in a criminal prosecution

direct examination... also called examination in chief by the party that called the witness. It is the asking of questions in court by the lawyer of a person called to testify as a witness

directed verdict... in a criminal case this is a verdict by the judge that the prosecution has failed to meet is burden and the case or some charges are dismissed or reduced to lesser included offenses

discovery...information, documents, exhibits and other things given by the prosecution to the defense in a criminal prosecution so that both sides will go to trial with as much information as possible. It will often include exculpatory information.

evidence...testimony or exhibits or other documents offered at trial and for use by the judge or jury to decide the case

eyewitness...a person who directly perceived or witnessed an event under discussion and can so testify in court at a trial or other hearing

felon...a person who has been convicted of a criminal offense usually punishable by more than a year in jail or penitentiary

felony...a crime which usually carries a minimum sentence of one year or more in state prison, as opposed to a misdemeanor which carries a sentence of one year or less and can often be served in a county jail

grand jury... a jury that hears evidence and decides if an accused person should be indicted and stand trial usually in a circuit court as opposed to a district court

hung jury... a jury that is unable to reach a unanimous verdict and is hopelessly deadlocked in a criminal case, it normally results in the judge declaring a mistrial and a new trial may or may not be started by the prosecution

hypothetical... a concession or assumption made for the sake of argument

indictment... the document which charges a person with a felony or serious crime and voted upon by the required number of grand jurors.

innocent... not guilty or without guilt

intentionally... a person acts intentionally with respect to a result or to conduct when his conscious objective is to cause that result or to engage in that conduct

juror... a person who is or has actually served on a jury

jury... a group of citizens called to hear the trial of a criminal prosecution and sworn to decide the facts or evidence in the case fairly and impartially, and to render a verdict in accord with the law as given by the judge

jury duty... being called to possible render service on a jury

jury box... the area reserved with seating for the jury

jury panel... the list from which jurors may be drawn for a jury trial

jury trial... a criminal prosecution in which the case is presented and the factual questions and final verdict are determined by a jury

kidnapping... a crime of restraining a person against their will by some method and holding that person for ransom or reward or to accomplish the commission of a felony or to inflict bodily injury or to terrorize the victim or to interfere with the performance of a governmental function or to use the person as a shield or hostage

misdemeanor...a crime punishable by one year or less (usually in jail) and a less serious offense than a felony

mistrial... an error or other irregularity in a criminal trial which results in premature termination of the trial. It might be based upon a deadlocked jury, statements by a witness. It may occur on motion by the judge or upon motion by one of the parties. The trial may have to begin again

murder...the most serious form of criminal homicide with homicide being defined as the crime of causing another's death

not guilty... the verdict after a trial by a judge and jury. It must be unanimous in all states except Oregon and Louisiana which allow 10 out of 12 jurors to reach a verdict

opening statements...a lawyers address to a judge or jury to outline what the evidence in the case will be

plea...the formal response to a criminal charge by a defendant. The possible pleas are guilty, not guilty, nolo contendere or an Alford plea

privilege against self incrimination, or taking the fifth...under the Fifth Amendment of the united States Constitution, the right of a defendant to refuse to give or make a statement, or to take the stand and testify in a criminal trial or proceeding

persistent felony offender (PFO)... sometimes called habitual offender means a person charged with a new crime is given a greater sentence based upon having been convicted of one or more crimes in the past within a stated period of time

presumption of innocence... a fundamental tenet and a constitutional protection afforded to every U.S. citizen accused of a crime, and which requires guilt to be proven beyond a reasonable doubt

prosecutor...the person that represents the state in a criminal proceeding. Also called commonwealth attorney, district attorney, county attorney or states attorney

rape...a crime of force in which the victim is made to have sexual intercourse (vaginal, oral, or anal) against their will or when consent is by unlawful means or the person is legally incapable of consent

reasonable doubt... the standard which the jury (or a judge in a non-jury case) uses in a criminal case to determine guilt or innocence. It is usually given as an instruction in every criminal case. Referred to as "proof beyond a reasonable doubt"

robbery...a crime of taking another persons money or other personal property by force, intimidation or threat of imminent harm. It is a felony in most states punishable by a term of years in the penitentiary. If a person is armed with a dangerous or deadly weapon, it is called armed robbery

search...an inspection of a person, place or thing usually by police or other law enforcement officers to reveal the existence of criminal activity or for the purpose of discovering evidence

self defense...use of force to protect yourself or a family member from bodily harm. Sometimes used as a legal defense to a crime of assault, battery or homicide and for which the law affords you an immunity or privilege

sodomy...a felony crime in most states and involves insertion of the penis in the mouth or anus of another person and usually accomplished by force and without consent, or with someone incapable of giving legal consent

stipulation...an agreement between the parties to a criminal case as to a fact or piece of evidence which simplifies the issues and eliminates calling of witnesses to prove that fact and the stipulated fact must be accepted by the judge or the jury

subpoena...an order of a court for a witness to appear at a particular time and place to testify or produce documentary evidence

summation, * see closing argument

theft... a word meaning all crimes ion which a person takes property of another without permission or consent and with the intent to make it their own or for their own use. In some states it has different degrees depending on the amount involve, for example over or under $100, $300, or $500. Also called petty theft, grand theft

trier of fact...the jury in a jury trial charged with deciding the facts of the case

verdict...the jury's decision in a case. In a criminal case it is required to be unanimous in all but two states

voir dire or jury selection... in a criminal jury trial the questioning of the jury panel or prospective jurors by the judge and or the attorneys for both sides at the begining of the trial

wanton...usually means grossly or extremely negligent or reckless. A person acts wantonly with respect or to circumstances when he is aware of and consciously disregards a substantial and unjustifiable risk that the result will occur or that the circumstances exist

witness... a person testifying under oath in a criminal trial. A person who sees an event

witness stand... a place where a witness sits next to the judge from which testimony is given usually into a microphone and videotaped, recorded or transcribed for the record

SUGGESTED READINGS

Adler, Stephen J. *The Jury: Trial and Error in the American Courtroom,* (Times Books, New York, 1994)

Aron, Roberto, Julius Fast, Richard B. Klein, *Trial Communication Skills* (McGraw-Hill, Colorado Springs, CO, 1986)

Burnett, D. Graham *A Trial By Jury* (Vintage Books, New York 2001)

Couric, Emily *The Trial Lawyers: The Nation's Top Litigators Tell How They Win*, (St. Martin's Press, New York, 1988)

Crawford, Dr. Richard J. *The Persuasion Edge: Winning Psychological Strategies and Tactics for Lawyers,* (Professional Educations Systems, Inc. 1989)

Dershowitz, Alan M., *Reasonable Doubts: The Criminal Justice System & the O.J. Simpson Case,* (Touchstone, New York, 1996)

Lief, Michael S., Caldwell, H. Mitchell, & Bycel, Ben *Ladies and Gentlemen of the Jury: Greatest Closing Arguments in Modern Law,* (Touchstone, New York, 1998)

Miller, Henry G. *On Trial: Lessons From A Lifetime In The Courtroom,* (ALM Publishing, New York, 2001)

Remington, Frederic & Charles M. Russell *Savvy Sayings: Lean & Meaty One Liners,* (Ken Alstad Company, Tuscon, AZ 1986)

Shapiro, Barbara J., *Beyond Reasonable Doubt and Probable Cause: Historical Perspectives on the Anglo-American Law of Evidence,* (University of California Press, Berkley, 1991)

Sonsteng, John & Robert Haydock, *Trialbook Second Edition.* (West Publishing Co. St. Paul MN 1995)

Wenke, Hon. Robert A. *The Art of Selecting A Jury*, (Parker & Son Inc., Los Angeles, CA 1979)

END NOTES

Introduction

[1] Allan M. Dershowitz, *The Criminal Justice System and the O.J. Simpson Case,* Simon & Schuster New York, (1996) pg 35.
[2] Bureau of Justice Statistics, Special Report, *Defense Counsel In Criminal Cases* by Caroline W. Harolow BJS Statistician, November 2000, NJC 179023.
[3] Now deceased University of Minnesota Law School Professor, Irving Younger, one of the country's leading experts on trial advocacy often said that no one could claim to be a good trial lawyer until he or she had tried at least 25 jury trials.
[4] Roberto Aron, Julius Fast, Richard B. Klein *Trial Communication Skills* McGraw-Hill, Inc. Colorado Springs, Co. (1986). Pg. vi.
[5] Emily Couric, *The Trial Lawyers: The Nation's Top Litigators Tell How They Won.* St Martin's Press, New York (1988) pg. 363.

Chapter One

[6] Todd Winegar, *The Ultimate Trial Notebook,* Salt Lake City, UT. 1996-1999. pg.1
[7] Todd Winegar, *The Ultimate Trial Notebook,* Salt Lake City, UT. 1996-1999. pg.1

Chapter Two

[8] Fred Lane, J.D. *Goldstein, Trial Techniques 2d ed.,* Wilmette, Illinois: Callaghan& Company, 1969. Vol 1., Chapter 10, pg. 3.
[9] Dr. Richard J. Crawford. *The Persuasion Edge,* Eau Claire, Wisconsin. Professional Education Systems, 1989. pg 104
[10] Fredric G. Levin. *Effective Opening Statements, The Attorney's Master Key To Courtroom Victory.* Executive Reports Corporation. Englewood Cliffs, New Jersey, 1987.
[11] Gerald N. Hill & Kathleen Thompson Hill, *The People's Law Dictionary.* New York, MJF Books, 1995. pg 295.
[12] Fredric G. Levin, *Effective Opening Statements,* pg iii.
[13] Sonsteng, John & Roger Haydock, *Trialbook Second Edition,* West Publishing Company, 1985 & 1995. pg 79.
[14] Todd Winegar, *The Ultimate Trial Notebook,* P.O. Box 353, Salt Lake City, UT 84110 © 1996-1998. Winegar provides an excellent Opening Statement Checklist that every attorney can follow in drafting an opening statement. Chapter 4, pg 1.

Chapter Three

[15] Michael S. Lief, H. Mitchell Caldwell & Ben Bycel, *LADIES AND GENTLEMEN OF THE JURY. Greatest Closing Arguments in Modern Law,* New York, Touchstone, 1998, pg 11.
[16] Henry G. Miller, Esq. *On Trial Lessons From A Lifetime In The Courtroom.* ALM Publishing, New York, 2001.
[17] Gerry Spence, *How To Argue and Win Every Time,* New York St. Martin's Press, 1995.

Chapter Four

[18] The 'Lectric Law Library's Lexicon on presumption of innocence. www.leclaw.com/def/i047.htm
[19] Adopted and proclaimed by General Assembly Resolution 217 A (III) of 10 December 1948.
[20] As amended by Protocol No. 11. Rome, 4. XI 1950.
[21] 2 Blackstone Commentaries. c. 27, margin page 358, ad finem.
[22] Quoting *Coffin v. United States* 156 U.S. 432, 453, 15 S.Ct. 394, 39 L.Ed. 481 (1895)
[23] Jury Instructions, Westlaw, Unofficial Transcripts 9/22/1995, pg 39.
[24] Senior Circuit Judge Hamilton, dissenting in United States v. Walton. Original panel opinion was unpublished. United States v. Walton 166 F3d, 336 4th Circuit 1998. Full text of opinion reproduced in United STates vs. Walton. Nos. 97-4498, 97-4537, 1998 WL 879650 (4th Circuit Dec 1998 (per curiam)
[25] This is the standard used primarily in civil cases.
[26] Civil cases involving moral turpitude, custody, libel, civil commitments often use this standard. See, e.g., *Gertz v. Robert Welch, Inc.,* 418 U.S. 323, 331-332 (1974).
[27] A standard used in denaturalization cases, deportation proceedings, and expatriation cases. See, e.g., *Woodby v. INS,* 385 U.S. 276 (1966); *Chaunt v. United States,* 364 U.S. 350 ((1960).
[28] The standard applied and used in criminal cases. See *In Re Winship,* 397 U.S. 358, 370 (1970) (Harlan, J., concurring).
[29] See *United States v. Fatico,* 458 F.Supp.388, 403 (E.D.N.Y. 1978), *aff'd,* 603 F.2d 1053 (2d Cir. 1970)

[30-31] *Reasonable Doubt and Probable Cause: Historical Perspectives on the Anglo American Law of Evidence,* Barbara J. Shapiro, University of California Press, 1991.

[32] See Anthony A. Morano, *A Reexamination o f the Development of the Reasonable Doubt Rule,* 55 B.U.L. Rev. 507, 513-15 (1975) Morano argues that prior to reasonable doubt there was the "beyond any doubt standard".

[33] 26 *State Trials*, 721, 811. They were also intstructed to convict if they believed the evidence.

[34] See Note #30-31

[35] *Commonwealth vs. Webster,* 59 Mass. (5 Cush), 320 (1850). This definition was widely adopted.

[36] *Reasonable Doubt: Interpretation and Enforcement* by Mark Davis, Junior Paper, Princeton University (Spring Paper) 2002.

[37] 397 U.S.358 , 90 S.Ct. 1068, 25 L.Ed. 2d 368 (1970).

[38] *United States v. Doyle*, 130 F.3rd 523 (2d Cir. 1997).

[39] Committee on Pattern Criminal Jury Instructions, District Judges Association, Sixth Circuit, Pattern Criminal. Jury Instructions § 1.03 (1991)

[40] For an excellent case with numerous references to defining and explaining reasonable doubt. see United States vs. Walton (3/27/2000) No. 97-4498, 97-4537, 1998 WL 879650 (4th Circuit Dec. 17, 1998 (per curiam)

[41] Again see, United States vs. Walton.

[42] Alan M. Dershowitz, *Reasonable Doubts: The Criminal Justice System and the O.J. Simpson Case.* New York, Simon & Schuster, 1996.

[43] Harry Toulmin and James Blair, *A Revision of the Criminal Law of the Commonwealth of Kentucky,* 2 vols. (Frankfort, KY, 1806, 2:317-318.

[44] Kentucky Criminal Rules (RCR 9.56)

[45] Again see, United States vs. Walton.

QUICK ORDER FORM

Fax orders: (502)589-6123

Email orders: chagan1@bellsouth.net

Postal Orders and fax orders will be sent by C.O.D. Please send this form

Please return this form:

NOT GUILTY EVERY TIME
Keys to Courtroom Victory

Name: _____

Address: _____

City: _____ State _____ Zip _____

email address: _____

Shipping by air:
U.S. $2.75 for first book and $2.00 for each additional book

International: $9.00 for first book, $5.00 for each additional book.